Radically Real!
The Quest for Authenticity

By David C. Weiss

Writers Exchange E-Publishing https://www.writers-exchange.com/

Radically Real!

Living As an Authentic Christian While the World Watches!

by Dave Weiss

Table of Contents

Acknowledgements

First of all I would like to acknowledge my Lord and Savior Jesus Christ. He has brought me through so many things, too countless to mention here, though several are alluded to in this book. He is the changer of hearts, the lover of souls and the ultimate Creative force in the Universe. Most importantly He is the only Son of God and the only way, not only to heaven but also to a truly complete life in the here and now.

Next, I would like to thank Chad Kinsey and Pastor Jim Bauer for their friendship and for reading over and editing my thoughts and helping me to write this vision more coherently.

To the members of B.I.G. and Mohrsville Church of the Brethren for putting up with me, supporting me and helping me to grow in Christ. Especially to Joe Elacqua and Corinne Woods for support, encouragement and a whole lot of fun.

To my sons Brandon and Chris for being the kind of sons any father would be proud of. These two guys had to be around while I learned a lot of this stuff the hard way. I am more grateful for you that you will ever know and I am proud to be your dad.

To my whole family for your love and support.

And to my wife Dawn, who led me to Jesus and loved me even when I wasn't all that loveable. I love you.

Introduction

When the Lord put it on my heart to write this book all the usual doubts reared their ugly heads. Who are you to write a book challenging the church? You're not the pastor of some huge church! Hey, come to think of it you're not the pastor of any church! You're not even shining as bright as many of the people around you. You don't have half the alphabet behind your name. You're just an ordinary guy! And the fact of the matter is that all those things are true. I am a person with some baggage, a person with a past and yet, here I am writing this book. Why? Because I feel the Lord tugging at my heart to do this. I feel Him asking me why the church has grown complacent (It's kind of a rhetorical question to get me to think, because I can assure you, He needs no knowledge from me). I feel Him asking me why we have lost our first love and are content with the counterfeit things the world has to offer? I feel Him saying that it is time for the church to wake up and get moving.

God has blessed me much more richly than I have ever deserved. I have let Him down countless times and yet He stuck it out and brought me through. I suspect many reading this book will identify with that statement. We have felt the amazing grace of a loving God in our lives. The question is do we live like it? Are we living like we have been saved by the grace of a loving God, or are we acting as if we earned salvation with our own goodness? Do we look at others with the kind of love that God looks at us with, or are we feeling just a little superior to them? If we are standing in a lineup of non-believers, could someone pick us out? Do the choices we make reflect well on our Father in heaven? When we say we are Christians, does our lifestyle make others want Christ?

Let me make one thing clear, this book will be as painful to write as it is to read. It is stepping on my toes even as I begin writing. That's OK. That is its purpose. This book is about seeking the face of God, seeking His will for your life. More specifically, it was written to challenge Christians to take a long, hard look at their lives and make whatever changes are necessary. It was written to challenge Christians to live a life that will help them to make a difference. It was written to help you to shine like a million-candle power spotlight in a dark world.

Jesus called us the light of the world. The world around us is full of despair. The things of the world are not filling the void in people's lives anymore. It is dark out there. Where is the light? People will be drawn to the light of Jesus like moths to a flame. People are starting to see that the artificial light that the world has to offer is really a bug zapper that brings destruction. But what is the alternative for them? The church has been so busy squabbling amongst themselves that the light has been growing dim. The church has grown too comfortable, closed itself in and stopped shining. Our light is under the bushel. It is time to shine! It is time to make a difference! It is time to be Radically Real!

Radically Real

Take my whole life
take all that I am
show me how I fit into
your marvelous plan.
Take the way that I look
and the way that I feel
turn me around.
Make me radically real.

Take all that you've given
and all that I've done
and make them shine bright
on my Savior, your Son
Use all of my talents
His truth to reveal
that you've changed my life
and made me radically real.

Take the good and the bad
take my whole life story
turn it around
to give you all the glory.
My sins you've forgiven,
my heart you have healed to tell of your love.
Make me radically real.

No pretense, no lies,
no ego, no pride
just a longing to share
what I'm feeling inside.
Not perfect, not holy,
not great, I'm assured,
just knowing there's heaven
with you as my Lord.
So take all I give
for as long as I live.
Your love that I feel
makes me radically real.

So take my whole life,
take all that I am
show me how I fit into
your marvelous plan
take the way that I look
and the way that I feel
turn me around,
make me radically real.

Chapter 1

What is Radically Real?

You are the salt of the earth. But if the salt loses its saltiness, how can it be made salty again? It is no longer good for anything, except to be thrown out and trampled by men.

You are the light of the world. A city on a hill cannot be hidden. Neither do people light a lamp and put it under a bowl. Instead they put it on its stand. And it gives light to everyone in the house. In the same way, let your light shine before men, that they may see your good deeds and praise your Father in heaven.

--Matthew 5: 13-16

There's an old saying. "If being a Christian was a crime, would there be enough evidence to convict you?" It's a question we must all ask ourselves. Are we living as Jesus would have us live? Are we being that salt and light that he called us to be or are we under the bushel, about to be trampled underfoot. Being Radically Real is being unquestionably Christian. It is the effort to be all you can be in Christ. It is living a life consistent with the teachings of Christ. It is about living a confident life full of the knowledge of Christ as your Savior. A Radically Real life is a life that brings honor and glory to God.

In the Bible, Christians are referred to as the children of God. The question is what kind of children are we? Are we the kind of children that our Father is proud to claim? Are we on the honor roll in the lessons of life or would we be the type that cause a long stream of stress and living lives that bring shame to our heavenly Father? Most of us, I believe live somewhere between the two points. At our best, people see our good works and praise our father in heaven and at our worst, people look at us in disgust and say, "And he calls himself a Christian." A Radically Real Christian is one who may struggle sometimes but is constantly striving to bring glory to his or her heavenly Father.

A WORD OF CAUTION...

We refer to God as our heavenly father for a reason. He is our father! Radically Real is not a prescription for perfection. All have sinned and fallen short of the glory of God. Even the best of us fall short frequently. Radically Real Christians realize this and know that at times they too will fall short. The question is, "What do we do about it when we fail?" Radically Real Christians fall on their faces and repent, asking God for forgiveness. They realize that they should not as Paul says, "sin so that grace may increase". But rather they seek to please God and bring him glory.

Some readers may look at this description and think that they are in no way shape or form good enough to be Radically Real. Congratulations, you are beginning to catch on. God's standard is perfection and we are all far from it. That is why we need Jesus, and salvation through His blood. If you are a parent, you will understand this more clearly. Do you love your children? (If you are not a parent, please bear with me for a moment, I think you will see where I am going with this.)

Do you love them when they do good? Do you love them when they make a mistake? Do you love them when they drive you crazy? Is there anything that could make you stop loving them? In most cases the answer is yes, I love them and nothing they could do will make me stop loving them. That is called unconditional love. If you, as an imperfect person, could feel that kind of love, imagine how the perfect creator of the universe must love you. It doesn't matter what you do God will forgive you, if you repent of it and ask him to. His love is complete and the blood of Jesus is enough to cover it all. Whatever you have done in your life, and no matter how long you have done it. No matter who you are and what you have and whatever other factors you can dream up, there is one thing you should never ignore and never forget. God loves you and He desperately wants to save you. Jesus traded the throne of heaven for a barren cross because He wants to save you.

He came that you might have life and have it more abundantly. He wants you to be Radically Real!

The world out there is looking for answers. The world is out there looking for people who know a better way. The world is doing everything it can to fill a hole that can only be filled by God. Drugs, alcohol, STD's, crime, immorality and a host of other social ills are not the disease, they are the symptoms of a society that has turned its back on God. The only cure for these symptoms is to return to God. Widespread revival brought on by the Holy Spirit working through Christians serious about the Gospel and salvation through Jesus Christ is what is needed. The world is groping in darkness for the light of Jesus Christ. They will examine Christians closely so we have got to be ready. We have got to be Radically Real! Are you up to the challenge?

Chapter 2

What Did Jesus Do?

The Ultimate Example of Radically Real

*Then Jesus declared, "**I am** the bread of life. He who comes to me will never go hungry and he who believes in me will never be thirsty."*

--John 6:35 (NIV)

*"**I am** the light of the world. Whoever follows me will never walk in darkness but will have the light of life."*

--John 8:12 (NIV)

*"**I am** the good shepherd. The good shepherd lays down his life for his sheep."*

--John 10:11 (NIV)

*"**I am** the resurrection and the life. He who believes in me will live even though He dies; and whoever believes in me will never die."*

--John 11:25 (NIV)

Thomas said to Him, "Lord, we don't know where you are going so how can we know the way?"

*Jesus Answered, "**I am** the way and the truth and the life. No one comes to the Father except through me."*

--John 14:6 (NIV)

Moses said to God, "Suppose I go to the Israelites and say to them, 'The God of your fathers has sent me to you,' and they ask me, 'What is His name?' Then what shall I tell them?"

*God said to Moses, "**I AM WHO IAM**. This is what you are to say to the Israelites, '**I AM** has sent me to you.'"*

--Exodus 3: 13,14 (NIV)

For God so loved the world that He gave His only begotten son that whosoever believeth in Him shall not perish but have everlasting life. For God did not send his Son into the world to condemn the world, but to save the world through Him.

--John 3:16, 17 (NIV)

Jesus...The Ultimate Example of Radically Real!

You've all seen it now, all that stuff with "WWJD?" on it. "What Would Jesus Do?" It is a great slogan and it should be the guide to decision making in the life of every Radically Real Christian. Really, though, it goes beyond that. I believe that as we look at, "What Would Jesus Do?", only half the story is told. The first question is "What <u>did</u> Jesus do?" It is vitally important that every Christian know this if they want to live the Christian life authentically. For the Christian, Jesus is our ultimate role model, a living breathing example of how we should live our lives.

As you look at the Scriptures listed in the introduction you see one thing very clearly, Jesus is the creator, sustainer and the source of life. He also provides the way to eternal life. It is important that we understand and believe this early on. Jesus is the Son of God, equal to God and the Holy Spirit, one third of the triune God-head, or Trinity if you will. There are people who do not believe this. They say that the word "Trinity" never appears in the Bible. I would respectfully submit that the word "Bible" never appears there either and yet we fully accept its existence. Jesus is God. For a time, He put on mortality and walked and lived among us to face what we face, lived the ultimate, righteous (sinless) life as an example to us and then gave His life for us. He was fully a man and He is fully God and His death on the cross was not the end of the story. He didn't remain on the cross and He didn't remain in the tomb. He rose from the dead and walked among the people for 40 days in which time He was seen by hundreds and thousands of people before he ascended into heaven. Believing this is the key to being a Christian.

God came and lived with us in Jesus. He gave us His word to point the way to Him and when we put our faith in Him He does mighty things through us and in us. Jesus Christ was and is the ultimate example of what it means to be Radically Real.

There are people that will always argue that Jesus was just a man. Love them, they are part of your mission field. You don't have to beat them over the head. Just love them and keep telling them. One thing that I have found that will stop a non-believer in their tracks is this statement:

Let's assume for a moment that Jesus was just a man, a good man, a great teacher, an all-around great guy. (This is really hard for me to do but for the sake of the lost, let's persevere.) His ministry on earth was for three years and then He died, period. Now think of all the millions and billions of people that have lived since then. Think of all the truly great people that have walked this earth between the cross and the turn of the millennium. Take any three-year period of the life of any one of them. Did they do enough to affect the whole world for 2,000 years? Has anyone in a three-year period ever had the impact that Jesus Christ has had? I think it is safe to assume that the answer will be no. I mean time itself is measured by his birth. One man with twelve main followers could never have had the impact that Jesus had on us in three years. However, one man who was really God, who continued working for all of the two thousand years very easily could. He is all powerful, all knowing, all seeing and his impact is felt in the world because He is still in the world; still working, still helping, still guiding, still leading, in short, still God. May his name be praised! Jesus is alive!!

To be a Radically Real Christian is to know Jesus in your heart; to have His Holy Spirit living and working in your life. It is a radical commitment to living His way, seeking His will, and reaching His lost sheep. It means giving Him every minute and every aspect of your life and letting Him do with it as He sees fit. It is having the faith to realize that the Creator of the universe, the one who knew His plan for your life before He made you, has the ability to guide your life far better than you ever could. So are you ready? Are you ready to make this commitment? Are you ready to be Radically Real?

In writing this book, I tried to look at the life of Jesus and the things he did as a pattern for the Christian life. I also looked at the adjustments we need to make in our own lives as we seek to follow him more completely. In truth, this book is incomplete. Every time I sit down to write and look to the Word of God, I become aware of even more that I should add. Will there be a sequel? I don't know. If God is willing, yes. However, the best thing I can recommend is that you do what I do. Read and study His Word and find the answers for yourself. Seek His Will in prayer and in all you do. I am writing this book with God's guidance and to the best of the ability he gave me, and my prayer is that it will be a blessing to those who read it. That being said, it will never be a replacement for the best guidance you could ever receive, the guidance of God and His Holy Spirit.

God will work in your life through His Word. Let Him. Now let's look at our Lord and Savior and our example of being Radically Real.

The chapters in this book are designed to look at things that Jesus did and then encourage believers to live His example. They also each contain a person or concept from the Bible that further expand upon the principles outlined in the chapter. This book has been the subject of much prayer and it is my hope that it will encourage the believer in His walk with the Lord. I am not, nor will I pretend to be a major league theologian. I am an imperfect person who has been saved by the blood of Jesus and is struggling beside you to be Radically Real.

Let's look at the example set by our Lord.

You Can Start Over

OK, I know what you're thinking Jesus had no need to start over. He never sinned. He had no need of forgiveness. That is all true. On the other hand, look how He treated people. Think about the way He dealt with the woman caught in adultery. The crowd was screaming for vengeance--for blood-shed. This woman was guilty as sin and the sentence was death. Jesus looked beyond that. He looked directly into the hearts of her accusers and saw all the impurity dwelling there. They wanted judgment for the woman without stopping to realize that they were equally in danger. Jesus gave those immortal words, "Let Him without sin cast the first stone." One by one the rocks hit the ground as the people walked dejectedly away. The woman cowering at the feet of Jesus looked around to see her accusers were gone. Jesus looked her in the eye and told her to, "Go and sin no more."

Two thousand years later, He is saying the same thing to you and me. He tells us to leave our sin behind and follow Him. We had a debt we could never pay, a debt of sin that would forever separate us from a loving God. Only one could pay the price and He did. He became the link between a righteous God and sinful man. He made it that you can start over.

A Free Gift That Will Cost You Everything

Jesus calls on us to be living sacrifices. Surely there can be no finer example of a living sacrifice than Jesus Christ. A few years back a singer named Joan Osbourne sang a song that asked the question, "What if God was one of us?" While I thought that song was a bit disrespectful to our Lord and not very biblical, the truth of the matter is that God was one of us. He left heaven to show us the way, to tell us the truth and to give us his eternal life. He was treated horribly at times and was crucified for His trouble. He knew that this would happen from before His birth and even though He prayed for another solution, when none was apparent, He put it all in the hands of the Father for you and me.

Sometimes people get caught up in the prayer at Gethsemane. They ask, "Why was he afraid if He already knew what the outcome would be?" The answer to this comes in the fact that He was fully man and fully God. As a man, He knew that this pain would be excruciating. Beatings with whips tipped with lead for maximum cutting power, nails through his hands and feet. Death by slow suffocation as the lungs could not fill properly while hanging in that fashion, the survival instinct causing a person to push against the nails through the feet to be able to get air into the lungs. This was going to be agony. As a perfect, sinless God, He knew that He would have to take on every sin that would ever be committed. I can almost assure you that this would have been almost unbearable even for a God. And yet He did it. He gave it all and sacrificed himself for us. Shouldn't we do the same for Him? In the same way that He experienced fear at Gethsemane, we experience fear at times in our walk, but we also know that through Him, we too will return to Heaven if we believe in Him. We know the outcome, we know that in the end we win, so let's keep pushing on to the prize.

Love Is the Key

The Bible tells us in John 15: 13 that, "Greater love has no one than this, that he lay down his life for his friend." This is exactly what Jesus did. The ultimate act of Jesus life was laying down his life for sinners such as us. But it's not just the sacrifice on the cross. It's not just His crucifixion. It is also the way that He laid aside His majesty, left Heaven and its adoring angels to come down to Earth to be mistreated, spat upon and murdered by sinful men. It is the way He submitted His will to the Father so that we might know Him and know the way to heaven. You may not be called to sacrifice your physical life for Jesus but it is clearly expected that we would lay aside our plans and ambitions and "Seek first the Kingdom of God, and His Righteousness".

Jesus told us a lot about love. He told us to love the Lord with all our hearts, and to love our neighbor as ourselves. But He didn't just tell us. He did it. He was filled with compassion for the people around Him. He went out of His way to help those in need. He healed the sick and the infirmed. He cast out demons. He showed mercy. He even fed them. He encouraged little children to come to Him, no matter how busy He was. The Bible tells us that God is Love and Jesus made that very clear in His life. He was and is an example of perfect love for us to model.

So how about you, are you going out of your way to model God's love? Jesus told us that people would know we are his followers by the way we love each other. Would people know that you are a Christian by the way you love them? If not, there is much work to do.

The Fight of Your Life

How are you holding up in the fight of your life, the fight against the enemy of your soul? In truth, none of us can hope to win that fight alone. We can only have victory in the fight by placing our trust in the one who came to save us. Do you feel like you have been taking a beating lately? Don't feel bad, look at what Jesus had to go through. His death on the cross had to look like a Satanic victory to His friends and disciples. Can you imagine the despair the disciples felt? They must have been totally demoralized and defeated. Can you imagine being Peter in that courtyard when he heard the rooster crow? Can you imagine the utter shame? And yet look what happened on the third day. Jesus rose from the dead. Jesus was who He said He was. Shame and pain and demoralization turned to victory. Jesus has a way of doing that for those who love Him.

Satan prowls around like a roaring lion seeking whom he might devour. He takes considerable joy in making the children of God forget who they are and cower in fear as he strikes at us. Don't fall for it. If you are a Christian, you are a child of the Most High God. Jesus Christ has already defeated Satan. Next time you feel like you are cowering in the face of Satan, run to Jesus and watch the devil cower for a change. In reality, on our own we are nothing but a little bug waiting to be stepped on by Satan. This is the fight of your life, if you want to win, Radically Real Christian, you have to go to the source of your life. We have to put on the armor He has provided take up the sword of His Word and rest in the knowledge that the battle really belongs to the Lord. In Him you can have victory in the fight of your life.

You Can Talk It...Can You Walk It?

Many people have lived good lives. Many people, by the world's standards, have lived good, moral, solid lives. Yet as we look at the Bible, we see that all have sinned and fallen short of the glory of God. Actually, that is not correct. There was one that didn't sin and fall short of the Glory of God and His name is Jesus Christ. This is why He was fit to be the perfect sacrifice for our sin. This is why He is our role model, the ultimate example of Radically Real.

So how can we do it? How can we "walk the talk"? In truth there is only one way: to give control of our lives over to Christ. After all, as the only one ever to pull off a perfect life, who better is there to guide us?

In the Bible, over and over again we see the Pharisees, talking it and not walking it. Before we get too tough on them, we need to be real with ourselves. Are we any better? Do we not often say one thing and do another? You see too often, we look at our status in the community, our righteousness and compare it with the folks around us and get to feeling a bit morally superior. We see our religious practices, our regular church attendance, our clean living and we start to feel high and mighty. We get a distorted view of ourselves because we look at ourselves in the broken mirror of a fallen world. How different are we really than the Pharisees? We need to cast that broken mirror aside and look at ourselves in the perfect mirror of Jesus to see where we come up short. It is in the perfect mirror of Jesus Christ that we will see how to be Radically Real!

Live It, Learn It, Love It

The Word of God: How many Christians use it the way they should? A Radically Real Christian's Bible should be worn out. It should be tattered, torn and marked up. The Word of God is one of very few things that look better with wear and tear. Are you in the Word the way you need to be?

Let's look at what Jesus did: When Jesus was in the desert being tempted by the devil (we'll look at this more in depth in a minute) what did he do? He quoted the Scriptures. He got out His two-edged sword (The Scriptures stored in His heart) and sliced and diced the arguments of His enemy.

When Jesus was confronted by the Pharisees, He often asked them, "What does the law say?" or "What do the scriptures say?" Jesus allowed His life to be guided by the Word of God. Jesus' life fulfilled the Word of God. Why? Because Jesus is God! Now if God in the flesh will live by the Word of God, shouldn't you? Of course you should. We have His Word on it! Again, I will ask the question, "Are you in the Word the way you need to be?"

Whose Are You?

Jesus stood in the presence of Satan himself. After going without food for forty days, one can imagine that Jesus was famished. Yet Jesus did not take advantage of the fact that He is God to turn the stones into bread, when He was tempted by Satan. He said, "man does not live by bread alone." When Satan turned up the pressure, He offered Jesus all the kingdoms of the world in exchange for His worship, Jesus turned Satan down flat. Satan took Jesus to the highest point of the Temple and told Him to throw Himself off. Now this could have been the greatest temptation of all for Jesus. The people were constantly disbelieving Jesus. A public spectacle such as gliding harmlessly from the precipice to the ground must have seemed awfully appealing, but the price was too high. He told Satan that it is written not to put the Lord your God to the test. Then Satan left Him. Three temptations on three different levels but always the same response, a quotation of the Scriptures and an unfettered obedience to God.

In our lives we face temptation every day. We face temptations on all different levels and how we face them tells us, and the world, a lot about our faith in God. How do you face them? The Bible tells us that there are really only two positions we can occupy when it comes to God. We are either for Him or we are against Him. There ain't a lot of room in the middle of the road here. Jesus tells us we can't serve two masters or we will end up hating one of them. The road is littered with the corpses of those who tried to dance on the yellow line. They got too close to the temptations of the world and they got run over by them. Which side of the road are you on? For the Radically Real Christian there can be only one answer, we must be on God's side. The temptation we face in our lives is small potatoes compared to the temptation that Jesus faced. I mean think about it, Lucifer fell and became Satan because He sought to wrestle the throne away from God. To win Jesus away from God would have allowed Him to secure Hs ultimate victory, the throne of God. You can bet that Satan threw everything He had at Jesus and Jesus stood strong and was obedient even unto death.

You might be saying, "Yes, but He was God." That would be true, but He is the same God who said that He would never leave us nor forsake us. If we stand with Jesus we can stand against any temptation. You see Satan's dirty little lie is that He is the opposite of God, that he is God's evil twin if you will. Nothing could be further from the truth. Satan is not the opposite of God. Satan is an angel, a being created by God. He is a powerful being, a being that can really mess you up, but he is certainly not all powerful. He might know how to get inside your head if you let him, but He doesn't know everything. As a matter of fact, we already know His future. In the book of Revelation, we see Him cast into the lake of fire forever. Radically Real Christians know that they are on the winning team. Who's team are you on?

Where Your Treasure Is

Bottom line, Jesus left His treasure in heaven and came down here to live a difficult life wandering from place to place. "Foxes have dens, but the Son of Man has no place to lay his head," He said. Jesus was here on a mission and the stuff of this world was going to do nothing but get in His way. He showed us by His example that God was of primary value, that people were next in line and that material wealth was nothing but things God gave for the purpose of serving His kingdom.

Think about it. Everything we have belongs to God if we have given our lives to Him. It is so vitally important that we follow Jesus' example in this. It becomes so easy for us to begin to serve the things that God has given us. What we should be doing is to serve Him with what He has given us. Too often the gifts He has given us to lay on His altar, end up getting altars of their own. Too often the blessings of God become "gods" to us. Whether it is material things, careers or anything else, if it gets between you and God it is nothing but a stumbling block to you. Jesus knew that. Jesus taught a better way. He taught us to lay up our treasures in Heaven, because where our treasure is, is where our heart will be. Doesn't it make more sense to store up our treasure where we will spend the most time? The 70 -100 years that most of us will get here are nothing compared to what eternity will be. Shouldn't we put our treasure in heaven? Shouldn't we invest our earthly treasure in seeing to it that many people will get to spend eternity in Heaven with us?

Jesus' example on possessions is one we all need to spend more time looking at, considering and modeling. There has never been a U-Haul behind a hearse. You can't take it with you so you might as well invest your earthly possessions in heavenly treasure!

Coming Out of the Prayer Closet

One of the biggest problems facing the body of Christ today is the comfort zone. We all have it. It is the safe happy confines of our church sanctuary. Now as the name "sanctuary" implies, the church should be a safe place for us to go to get away from the world. How can that be seen as a problem? Only when our faith is hung on a hook and left there to wait the week until we return. We have got to stop being closet Christians! We have got to leave the comfort zone and step out in faith to do the work of the Kingdom. There is no greater example of this than Jesus.

Think about it. Where is it more comfortable than Heaven? Isn't the comfort of Heaven (in the presence of God) the ultimate reward of every Christian? Jesus was there and came here. Jesus knew without Him we are hopeless and so He left the comfort of Heaven to experience birth and childhood and adolescence and temptation and pain and persecution and death so that we might be saved. Jesus left His comfort zone to do the work of the Father. Are we called to do any less?

If It Ain't Broke

Jesus challenged people to go against the status quo and make a difference. Think about it. The people were mistreating the Temple by turning it into a marketplace, where animals were sold for sacrifice at exorbitant fees. People were coming to worship God and being ripped off in the process. It had probably gone on like that for years but Jesus came and cleared the Temple. It may have gone on that way before, but things were going to be different now.

Jesus challenged the status quo in His teachings as well. He told us that the world taught to love our friends and those who love us back. Jesus told us to love our enemies and pray for those who persecute us. He taught us mercy over the law. He taught us by His example that we were to reach out to people without regard to social status or past sins. He taught us to meet people where they are. He taught us that it is not enough to accept Him and then sit idly by and wait for heaven. Jesus challenged the attitudes of the religious elite. He showed us that following Him and doing the will of the Father is not always the easy way, but it is always the right way. Far too often we see our comfort as a sign of God's blessing, but He shows us that sometimes if it ain't broke we need to break it. We need to push past the conventional wisdom to seek His wisdom. We need to be willing to follow His example. We need to put it all on the line to make changes, not for the sake of change but for the sake of reaching the lost.

Let It Shine

Who left their light shine more than Jesus? I mean think about it, a sinless God living among us. So why did they hate him so much? Why does His name, even today, cause so much controversy? To paraphrase noted "theologian", and former Van Halen lead singer, David Lee Roth, "If you walk through life with your head above the crowd, sooner or later someone is going to throw a rock at it." Jesus lived a totally perfect life. Perfection is scary to people. When they see it, they try to throw mud at it, they want to cover up the light. If we live our lives to glorify God and not ourselves, we cannot help but shine. Some people will love us and admire us, but many will hate us just like they hated Jesus. So, the question is, "Who are you going to serve?" The Bible tells us that there are those who live their lives as unto men and they have their reward. Glorification from men is all the reward they will ever receive. That is nowhere near enough for the Radically Real Christian. We live to hear the creator of the Universe say, "Well done good and faithful servant enter into your reward!"

Why are we to let our light shine? Why are we to be out there, out in the open, being Radically Real? The answer is to glorify God! Who glorified God more than our Lord and Savior, Jesus Christ? Think about when Jesus was at Lazarus' tomb. Do you remember what he said when he prayed aloud before raising Lazarus from the dead? He said, "Father, I thank you that you have heard me. I knew that you always hear me, but I said this for the benefit of the people standing here, that they may believe that you sent me." (John 11: 41,42 NIV) Jesus could have just said, "Lazarus, come out" but that would have focused the glory on His own power. Instead by praying aloud, Jesus gave glory to the Father and credibility to His Claim of being the Son of God. If the Son of God, who is in fact God, cared about glorifying God before men, how much more should the Radically Real Christian see to it that God is glorified in any good thing we do?

Jesus healed the sick. Jesus cast out demons. Jesus walked on water. Jesus did many extraordinary things, but Jesus was always careful to make sure that the glory was always carefully placed where it belonged. In the same way, God will give you as a Radically Real Christian, opportunities to shine. He will give opportunities to do things that will be recognized by men as wonderful and worthy of recognition. It is always crucial to remember that it is God who provides the abilities, the circumstances and everything needed to do all the good that we do. Since he provided everything doesn't he deserve the Glory for our actions?

Sometimes He will also give us opportunities to shine in the darkness, which people will not appreciate at all. Our light shining will shine the light on the evil being done by others. We might be shunned or face persecution. Is that any excuse for not shining? Absolutely not. We need to look no further to our Lord and Savior, the sinless lamb of God hanging on the Cross, to see that we must shine in all the circumstances, those that bring adoration and those that bring persecution and maybe even death. After all we are not shining for man's glory, we are shining for God's glory. We are not shining for an earthly reward; we are shining for a heavenly reward. The world may not like our light, they may not like the way that they look when we shine on them, but then again, what can the world really do to a Radically Real Christian? We can shine confidently, knowing that with Jesus as our Lord and Savior, the persecutions are temporary and the reward is eternal. There is amazing power in knowing Jesus. Use His power to shine bright.

To be a Radically Real Christian there is no substitute for walking with Jesus. There is no substitute for doing what Jesus did. We have a powerful weapon in our arsenal in the Word of God. In the Word we can learn by example from what Jesus himself did. Any situation we face can be answered with the wise counsel of the Word of God. There is no question about it, Jesus is our ultimate example. Now let's look more closely at what it means to follow Him. Let's look at what it means to be Radically Real.

Chapter 3

You CAN Start Over!

Radically Real Conversion

Now there was a man of the Pharisees named Nicodemus, a member of the Jewish ruling council. He came to see Jesus at night and said, "Rabbi, we know you are a teacher who has come from God. For no one could perform the miraculous signs you are doing if God were not with him.

In reply, Jesus declared, "I tell you the truth, no one can see the kingdom of God unless he is born again."

"How can a man be born when he is old?" Nicodemus asked. "Surely he cannot enter a second time into his mother's womb to be born!"

Jesus answered, "I tell you the truth, no one can enter the kingdom of God unless he is born of water and the Spirit. Flesh gives birth to flesh, but the Spirit gives birth to spirit. You should not be surprised at my saying, "You must be born again. The wind blows wherever it pleases. You hear its sound, but you cannot tell where it comes from and where it is going. So it is with everyone born of the Spirit."

--John 3:1-8 (NIV)

The first step in your pursuit of being a Radically Real Christian is obvious. You have to be a Christian. You have to have a personal relationship with Jesus Christ. You have to have asked Jesus into your heart to be your Lord and Savior. Jesus came into this world to save us from our sin. The blood He shed on the cross saves us from the fires of hell. In John 14: 6, Jesus said, "I am the way and the truth and the life, no man comes to the Father but through me. (NIV)" I don't think he could have been any clearer. If you want to get to the Father in Heaven, you have to go through Him.

If you haven't made the decision to invite Jesus Christ into your heart to be your Lord and Savior, now is the time. It is the most important, best decision you will ever make. In our society today, we are always apt to put things off 'til tomorrow. Don't fall into that trap. None of us are guaranteed tomorrow. You could be run over by a truck the next time you cross the street. You could be struck by lightning. You could even just fall over while you're reading this book. Would you be ready if that were the case? Are you ready to meet your maker? Ask yourself these questions:

Can you remember a specific time when you asked Jesus into your heart?

Do you believe that Jesus is the Son of God?

Do you believe that He died for your sins?

Do you believe that He rose again?

Are you sorry for your sins and want to try to do better?

If you answered no to any of those questions, you need to do some heavy thinking and praying. You need to ask Jesus into your heart! Don't tell me you believe in God. The devil can say that much. Don't tell me you go to church. You can warm a pew your whole life and not get into Heaven. Don't even tell me you read your Bible and pray. All those things are great and important and they will help you in life but without a saving faith in Jesus Christ, Heaven is impossible. Sin cannot enter into the presence of God and without the cleansing through Jesus' blood you cannot go to the Father. The Bible says, "All have sinned and fallen short of the glory of God." (Romans 3: 23) That means you, me and everyone else has sin in their life and needs a Savior. The Bible also says this "The wages of sin is death, but the gift of God is eternal life in Christ Jesus our Lord." (Romans 6:23)

You see, sin requires a price and the price is death. In Old Testament times, animals were sacrificed and their blood was shed as a price for sin. When Jesus came, He came to take away our sin once and for all. That's why they call Him the Lamb of God. He died to take away your sin and mine. When they made a sacrifice, the lamb had to be without defect. Likewise, Jesus was without the defect of sin. He was the perfect "lamb" to be sacrificed to take away your sin and mine. He came to be your Savior. Is He? If you are not sure, now is the time to be sure. God gave us free will. He will never force you to accept His free gift. You will have to ask. If you would like to ask Jesus into your heart, I invite you to do it right now. Simply pray this prayer and mean it with all your heart:

Heavenly Father,
I know I am a sinner.
I know that I don't always live the way you would have me live
And I'm sorry. Lord, please forgive me.
I want to do better.
Thank you for sending your Son to Die for me,
And thank you that He rose again.
Lord Jesus, come into my heart and be my Lord and Savior
Give me your Holy Spirit as my guide and
Help me to live each day as you would have me live.
You gave your life for me,
I give my life to you.
Thank you Lord, In Jesus Name
Amen

If you just prayed that prayer for the first time, Welcome to the family of God! You have just made the best decision you have ever made. There are a few important things you must now do:

1. Find a solid, Bible believing church. We need the help and encouragement of other believers especially in the beginning of our walk with the Lord. We also need to worship the Lord. He is worthy!

2. Get a Bible and read it. If you have never read before, I recommend starting with the book of John, as opposed to reading cover to cover. I say this for two reasons:

- The book of John covers almost every aspect of the Christian Faith.

Many readers get bogged down in the Old Testament books, especially Leviticus and Numbers. While these books are full of crucially important information, they can be difficult to comprehend.

- I also recommend that you get a translation of the Bible such as the New International Version. The language is much easier to read for the beginner. And one last thing, when you read, really read! Take notes, study, reread and most importantly pray that God will show you how what you are reading applies to your life.

3. Find a friend that will help you to stay accountable. This should be a person that is a Christian (preferably a Radically Real one) who is not afraid to tell you when you are off the mark.

4. PRAY DAILY!!! And never give up.

There's more good news. God is not just the God of the afterlife. He is God of now, too. Jesus came so that we might have life and have it more abundantly. That means not only do we have eternal life, but God will give meaning to our lives here on earth as well. I am about to tell you the story of a man I know and the changes Jesus Christ has made in his life.

A Second Chance!

We'll call him "Bob." Bob was a guy not long out of high school. He was a decent person although fitting in was not something he was particularly good at. He graduated and immediately (one month later) went to a trade school far from home to try his hand at pursuing the American dream. A recruiter from the school had convinced Bob that people in his chosen profession regularly earned as much as $80, 000 per year. Having never really been accepted by his peers and often abused by them, Bob was a young man with something to prove. He remembers thinking that he could finish this school in three years of concentrated study and be well on his way to six figures while his abusers were still flipping burgers. That and the fact that Bob and his parents had the usual disagreements, that seem almost insurmountable at the age of 17, led Bob to go 400 miles from home for a course of study for which he had no aptitude. About two weeks before he left for school, Bob got his first "real" girlfriend and of course he pined away for her most of his time in school. While Bob had dabbled with alcohol a few times in high school, it was not until the last weekend before leaving for school that he got drunk for the first time. Not just a small buzz either as he tells it, but the kind of drunk with violent illness that made him stay away from alcohol his whole time at school.

Bob's relationship with God was almost non-existent. He went to catechism, because that's what all the other kids his age did, he got confirmed and he left the church. By the time he left for college, he had not set foot in a church except for weddings and funerals in nearly five years. He had little regard for the people in the church, regarding them as hypocrites who were trying to make themselves feel better by looking for sin in other peoples' lives. He cited one incident in trade school where one of his three roommates (who drank, swore and did all the same stuff everyone else did) borrowed his car to go to church and hit a car with it on their apartment parking lot and drove off as if nothing happened. Bob was working as a closer at a fast-food restaurant at the time and was awakened by a police officer Sunday morning. It soon became apparent what had happened and even though his roommate made good on the damages, Bob had yet another reason to see no need for church or God. To Bob, God was for the televangelists to scream about as they were bilking old ladies out of their social security checks (That was his impression at the time). As far as Bob was concerned, he only knew very few people to whom God seemed to make a real difference. Chief among them was his grandmother who always tried to get him to go to church, and told him she was praying for him. He knew she was sincere, and he loved her, but he figured she was just someone who had been fooled by old traditions.

College was taking its toll on Bob. He started out with good grades, but the distance from home and a lack of discipline and aptitude soon took care of that. He began working at the previously mentioned fast food restaurant, and started eating most of his meals there. Pizza delivery was his chosen meal at the apartment and with no more track meets to inspire him to run and stay in shape, Bob was quickly gaining weight. He had made a few lasting friendships but for the most part he was lonely and depressed. The distance from home made it difficult to get back to his family and the girlfriend he left behind. After the first year, Bob left school and returned home.

Home was no better. The girlfriend was gone, and the friends Bob had left at school were now the ones Bob was missing. With dreams, but no real marketable skills Bob ended up bouncing from fast food job to fast food job, flipping the same burgers his former classmates were but with no light at the end of the tunnel. It was about at this time that Bob rediscovered alcohol. He eventually landed a depressing job at a factory that put him on second shift, "the drinker's shift." Even though he was underage, he found places in the small town that didn't care as long as his money was green and now he could drink from 11 p.m. until 2 a.m. Then he would sleep it off and start the whole cycle all over again.

He had a few failed relationships, which made him more and more depressed which made him drink more. Before long, if Bob was not an alcoholic, he was well on his way. He began to find no hope at all in his life. He hated working in the factory. The folks from his high school class were beginning to land good jobs and he was stuck. By the age of 22, Bob could see very little point of going on. Thoughts of suicide were a regular occurrence. In short, Bob was nearing the end.

He still remembers the night it all changed like it was yesterday. Having abandoned any hope long ago, he decided that this would be his last night. He wanted to spare his parents the stigma of having a kid who committed suicide so he decided he would get real drunk, go out and drive real fast and let nature take its course. He left the bar and began driving at speeds of over 80 miles per hour on the curvy back roads near his home. He almost lost it a few times but somehow, he held on. Then something weird happened. As he drove, he began to see things. He began to see all the people he loved mourning over him. It was weird for him because the thoughts he was having were more like visual images than idle thoughts and they led him to an inescapable conclusion. He didn't want to die. He just could not go on living the way he was. He pulled the car over and cried out the simplest of prayers, "God help me." Those three words changed his life forever. As he describes it, it's almost as if God was there right behind him with a band of angels just waiting for him to come to the conclusion, and as soon as the three words were said, God said, "close enough boys, go get him."

Within two weeks after that night, his sister introduced Bob to a girl she worked with. Now although Bob's sister had no idea about his "fateful" night, she knew he was in trouble. She thought this girl would be good for him. She failed to mention a few things about this girl, but we will get to that in a minute. They scheduled a double date for the following weekend at a nice safe amusement park. Bob was happy with this because there would be beer available in case he got nervous (he had not yet gotten over drinking). He remembers his sister telling him, "she doesn't drink and she won't like it if you do." That and the fact that he was with his sister and her boyfriend who he didn't yet trust with "his little sister" made him realize he was going to have to "do this date sober".

He met the girl the night before they went out for the first time at a fire company carnival (he was a volunteer fireman working at one of the games). He liked her right away, but there was something different about her. That night, as they were cleaning up the carnival, he was talking with his buddies about his big date the next day, one guy came up and said words Bob will never forget. "Bob, you know that girl you're going out with tomorrow night, her dad is a MINISTER." (That would be the fact Bob's sister conveniently left out if you are keeping score.) Bob at first said something to the effect of "Get the (expletive deleted) out." The guy was serious. Bob panicked. By this time, he hadn't set foot in a church in about seven or eight years and in about twelve hours he was going to pick up the "preacher's daughter". How would he explain himself to this "pious man of God"? Bob expected this man to judge him swiftly and "cast him out".

The day he picked her up, Bob got a reprieve. Her dad wasn't home and all Bob had to deal with was her demon possessed German Shepherd. Bob thought it strange that a minister would have a pet possessed of the devil and yet there he was, a hundred and twenty pounds of snarling teeth. Bob also thought it funny that this hound of hell was named Shadrach after the guy in the Bible. Having gotten past the gatekeeper, (OK, she came out and yelled at the dog and walked to the car, Bob was a lot of things but not crazy) they went out on their date and had a great time. The following week, Bob met her father and a strange thing happened, the judgment was not there. The man was genuine, down to earth, kind and even sort of funny. He accepted Bob from day one. When Bob said something biblically incorrect (as he did often), her dad would simply show him or tell him kindly, in the most unthreatening way, where it was in scripture and "explain it in clear terms anyone could understand".

One day, the girl asked Bob to go to church with her. This was something Bob was pretty sure he was not ready for but he finally gave in. A weird thing happened. He liked the service. The pastor made the Bible come alive. His message seemed "strangely clear and rational". Bob started to want to go to church. He was learning and enjoying himself. Was there really something to his "grandma's God"?

Sunday school presented another problem. Here he would have to read in front of the class from time to time. This made him nervous which made him stammer. He was learning but as he tells it some of his beliefs were still "a little bit out of left field." No one mocked him or put him down, they just tried to show him a different way, the right way. They were willing to accept him too. One night at a revival service, (These crazy people went to church on weeknights, too) it was different. The church was full but it was as if the preacher was speaking just to Bob. When he gave his altar call, Bob was the first one forward and accepted Christ as his Lord and Savior. A few months later Bob popped the question and married the girl.

It's almost 15 years later now and they are still happily married. They have two sons who are Bob's pride and joy. Bob and his wife are deacons in the church. Bob, the guy that used to be afraid to read aloud in front of the Sunday school now fills in and preaches from the pulpit. He is in his church's ministry training program and hopes to become an evangelist. His years of self-inflicted pain are replaced with the joy of knowing all things are possible through Christ. Bob had a second chance. Bob is born again.

Make no mistake about it. On the night Bob tried to end his own life, he succeeded. He came to the realization that he could not live that life another second. He came to the end of himself and fell at the feet of God. The changes in his life were not instantaneous in fact some were painfully slow. But God in his own time changed Bob's life and today all the stuff that happened in Bob's life is what he uses to lead others to Christ. Bob's life verse is Romans 8:28: "In all things, God works for the good of those who love Him who are called according to His purpose." Bob tells it this way. "There is nothing in your life that God can't use to help someone. Nothing! But first you have to give it all to him."

A New Lease on Life!

The next man in our story we will call Frank. Frank was a young married man. A new Christian, Frank was trying to do all he could. His father was the sole breadwinner in his family and this allowed his mother to care for him and his brother and sister full time. Frank wanted the same for his young family, but his work as a commercial artist was nowhere near enough to do this. Frank reasoned that art was his God given talent; he had always had it since he was three years old. Surely this was God's chosen path for him and if he just worked hard enough and was faithful, God would bless him and make him prosperous enough to be the kind of breadwinner his dad was. Frank was driven and determined. He would work his day job as an advertising layout designer and then freelance at night for a variety of companies. In his spare time Frank was always trying to design the next big cartoon sensation. Frank would work as many as 12 to 15 hours a day, every day. He took a lot of pride in that. But Frank was not succeeding. Jobs would fall through. Clients would refuse to pay for finished work or delay payments for months.

Frank was having huge disappointments in life, too. He and his wife had one son who he loved very much. Frank thought about the way his brother and sister had been such an influence on his life and he wanted to give his son siblings. Frank's wife became pregnant and he was overjoyed. When his wife miscarried, Frank consoled himself with the fact that they were young and they could try again and then buried himself in his work 'til the pain went away. Then they had a second miscarriage. Frank began to blame God for the things that were happening, but at least he had his work. By the time his wife became pregnant for the third time, Frank was working 18 to 20 hours a day. His day job was a nuisance that kept Frank from pursuing his dream. His family would be OK once he "made it" and then he would have time for them. After all, the really successful people in his field were becoming millionaires. Surely if he worked a little harder God would start blessing him again. "God helps those who helps themselves and who is helping themselves more than me," he would say.

This pregnancy was different, however. At the tenth week, when they went to the doctor, the baby's heart was beating. They were finally going to have another baby. As Frank tells it, when he saw that little flutter on the screen, he cried like he had never cried before. By the time Frank's baby was born, the company he worked for full time had deteriorated and was downsizing. Frank lost his job the day the baby was born. "It's OK," he told himself, "Now I can pursue my dream full time and besides we couldn't afford day care anyway." God was opening doors. Frank decided to become a full-time freelancer. Frank became "Mr. Mom". Frank got a rude awakening. Babies are not easy to begin with and this baby was not an easy baby. He vomited every day for almost a year and a half. He didn't sleep through the night for over a year. Frank rarely got to do more than an hour or two of work while his wife was at work, and then he couldn't stay up half the night like he did before because as soon as he would get to sleep, the baby would wake up.

Frank's clients were another story, some came through and paid on time, but most either stuck him with bills all together or waited months and months to make payment. Frank and his wife were running up a huge debt on their credit cards to buy groceries, formula and diapers. During that period of time Frank also lost two very important people in his life. Frank held true to his pattern and just worked harder, and buried his pain in his work. "Where is God? Why is he letting me struggle like this?" Frank thought.

Finally, after a year and a half, it was clear that Frank had to go back to work. He took a job as a stock clerk at a department store figuring that after a few months' work would pick up and he could return to his freelance work full-time. He hated the job because it was not artwork, his God-given talent after all. He considered himself a failure and a loser. Although he worked a lot as his baby grew, he was still not succeeding and when a management position was offered in the store he took it. The job was demanding. Seventy-hour weeks for an 18,000 dollar a year salary as he tells it. He still managed to make time to work on his art, because all else was failure. Church attendance was often preempted by work but even when it wasn't Frank was too bitter at God to really concentrate. Frank, in an act of desperation, took a pay cut to take an art job. He was downsized from that job in a matter of six months, and he ended up in a sales position. Now he spent most of his time on the road, living in hotels a week at a time. There was rarely time to work on his art. Frank describes it as a time when he was dying spiritually. He felt as if God had abandoned him.

One day, as he was driving to his next sales call, a strange thought had occurred to him. "Your work is your god." He tried to shake it but it grew and he couldn't ignore it. The thought was right. His son was almost 16 and he hardly knew him. The baby he prayed for, for all those years was almost three, and he hardly had time for him. His marriage was disintegrating fast and why? Not because God had failed, but because Frank had failed. Frank failed to tend to what was really important in life. Frank put everything behind his career.

Frank had, at the suggestion of his wife, signed up to go to some event with the pastor and a couple of guys from church. It was something from Promise Keepers called "Stand in the Gap." It was truly the most amazing thing that Frank had ever seen. Well over a million men were there that day all praising and glorifying God in peace and love. Frank listened to the speakers intently. One after another they spoke, challenging the multitude to go out and be better husbands, better fathers, better citizens, and most of all better Christians. Frank describes it this way, "It was as if each of the speakers were speaking just to me. It was as if God got all those guys together just so he could talk to me. God tore down all the walls that day. I cried more than I have cried in my whole life."

One thing that spoke to Frank the most was when the speaker had the men praying face down in the dirt. He told each man to take out his wallet, take out a photo of someone he had wronged and pray for that person. "I only had two photos in my wallet, my wedding picture and a picture of my sons," Frank recalls "that was all I needed. As I looked at their faces I became totally convicted that I was wronging them and only serving myself by continuing my career pursuit. As the tears began to fall I realized that I needed to change and fast." Then when they stood the men up, Frank was supposed to pray with the other men from his church. He confessed it all to them through his tears and they vowed to help him do better. They held to that promise.

Frank came away from that day a new man. Jesus Christ so radically changed him that it took his family a little while to get used to it. Frank had a new sense of purpose. He had a longing to serve God. He laid his precious career on the altar and left it there. He found a new purpose. The senior high Sunday school teacher had stepped down and they needed a replacement. Frank signed up for the job. A few months later he restarted the youth group at his church. At first there were quite a few nights where Frank was alone, no kids having shown up. Today his group is over 15 kids. Frank is also now in training for the ordained ministry and feels called to evangelism. Frank now uses his art talent for the good of the kingdom and as he describes it, "it's fun again." Frank has become a Radically Real Christian. When Frank had the chance to start over, he took it. God allows "u-turns". If you need one, take it.

Bob and Frank both show us something very important. They show us that if we want to be Radically Real, we must all eventually come to the end of ourselves and look up to God. Bob needed to leave the bars behind and look to God to be his comforter. Frank needed to realize just because his talent and ability were God-given did not mean that he could serve them rather than God. Also take note that both Frank and Bob needed the help of other Radically Real Christians. Bob's wife and in-laws modeled true Christianity to him and it saved him. The men of Frank's church were there to support him as he made radical changes (and difficult ones). They were there to keep him accountable. Frank especially had one friend who took the time to sit with him and help him "shoulder the load." If you are struggling in this area, I encourage you to find someone who will be straight with you to be an accountability partner, someone who will be brutally honest with you when you need it.

It is at this point that I must confess something. Bob and Frank are not really two different men. Bob and Frank are the same guy at two different points in his life. Bob represents the early days of his life, the days before he knew the Lord, the days of struggle to fill the God-shaped hole in his life. All the things he tried led him further and further down a destructive path until he literally had two choices, death or looking to God. Frank represents the period in his life after he got saved where he became confronted with many realities of life and chose the wrong path. Frank is represented in the Bible in the parable of the sower. Frank's faith was like the seed sown among the thorns. The pressures of life very quickly choked out his faith like thorns choke out young plants. Frank once again was trying to fill the God-shaped hole. Once again, the same conclusion is reached. Like the square peg that can never fill the round hole, no one but God can fill the God-shaped hole. Frank almost lost all the things God had blessed him with before he figured that out.

How do I know so much about Bob and Frank? Because "their" real name is David Weiss. I am the guy who did all that stuff. Why do I share all this in a book I truly hope will be read by a lot of people? Because I want you to know beyond the shadow of a doubt that God will change your life. Jesus said he came that we might have life and have it more abundantly. It is 100% true. Someone cared enough to throw me the life rope of Jesus Christ. These people were Radically Real Christians. It is my hope that people will read this book and go about the business of throwing the rope to the hurting in this world and help to pull them to the solid ground of salvation. I also hope that someone might see my story and realize that there is hope in Jesus Christ. People like I was are out there in droves living in the darkness looking for someone to bring them light. This sounds like a job for the Radically Real.

One last thing, if you are a person in the Bob and/or Frank stage of your life I have some advice. Nothing in this world will fill the space that was made for God. Don't even try anything else it will not work. Oh, it may feel good for a while, but it is a cheap counterfeit of what God has to offer. God's plan for your life will be better than anything else you can try. It has to be, it is perfect. And once you are working on His plan, your life will be complete. Pray for guidance and then get moving. He will lead you the right way. If you make a mistake He will set you straight.

Another thing I touched on about the Bob/Frank periods was depression. Depression is a monster that will eat you up from the inside out if you let it. Depression will also make you resign yourself to things that you can fix. Depression made me resign myself to the "fact" that I was a loser and that my situation was the best it would ever be. Depression also makes you look for a way out. Depression made me turn to alcohol. Depression made me bury myself in a futile career. Depression almost made me take my own life. Depression is a tool of the devil and it is a powerful one. It makes you lose hope. It makes you lose your will power. It may even cause you to lose your resolve to seek God and His Will for your life. In my case, it almost made me leave this world without Jesus. I would be in Hell today were it not for God's intervention in my life.

Later, depression also, almost destroyed my witness. I was a Christian but the way I was living would never have appealed to anyone. I was useless to the kingdom and the Devil was excited and happy about it. I was allowing him to mess with God's plan for my life. If you are in depression today, there is hope! You are a child of God. God has a plan for your life. It is perfect and it's high time you started to live it. I am going to tell you now what worked for me. I am not a psychologist, and no doubt some of them would argue with me, but I believe that if you try this "technique" it will change your life.

When I was in the Frank stage of life my Sunday school teacher was a man named Dale. Dale is a brilliant man of God but he used to aggravate me. As a psychologist and minister, he would often go into the topic of depression. He used to always say that, "depression was caused by people who looked at the whole world as it affected them, selfishly." When I was depressed, this would make me crazy. How could he know what I was going through? Remember earlier in this paragraph when I said Dale was brilliant. He is! And he was 100% right. Once I turned the focus from myself to helping others, the depression went away. I could see the world as more than just how it affected me. That perspective changed my life. If you are struggling with depression, I wholeheartedly suggest that you try volunteering or just try to help someone who needs it. I think you will find that it will make all the difference and in the process you will be doing something Radically Real.

Radically Real Examples from the Bible

Nicodemus

"You must be born again." Jesus is speaking clearly and concisely, but what does He mean? That's what Nicodemus is up against, that and a lot of other things. You see Nicodemus has a problem. He is a very powerful man. He is a Pharisee, one of the leaders of the synagogue. He is a scholar, probably an expert on scripture and a highly regarded member of society. There is a better than even chance that he makes a handsome living being a Pharisee. Along comes Jesus, and like so many other people Nicodemus' comfortable life is turned upside down.

This man, Jesus, was attracting quite a following, and this was very disturbing to the Pharisees. In the scriptures, over and over again, we see the Pharisees trying to catch Jesus in something they can incriminate Him with. He was after all, claiming to be the Messiah and surely this man was no Messiah, they thought. Out of strict adherence to God's law (which in truth wasn't that strict because they kind of picked and chose what they followed), man-made tradition and their own self-righteousness, the Pharisees felt they needed to silence Jesus and do it fast.

We don't know for sure exactly how it had happened. Perhaps Nicodemus was out trying to find some dirt on Jesus, listening to him and waiting for him to make a mistake. Perhaps Nicodemus heard all that was going on and checked the scriptures and saw that Jesus was fulfilling prophecy after prophecy but in some way Nicodemus became convinced that Jesus was exactly who he said he was. Now that he had this information, what would he do with it? To become a believer would cost him his position, his livelihood, his standing in the community and basically everything he had worked for his whole life. What could he do?

So convinced of Jesus' righteousness and the fact that He was from God, Nicodemus boldly proclaimed it from the pulpit of the temple, right? No, he had a somewhat clandestine meeting with Jesus late at night, somewhere out of the way where no one would have to know about it. Nicodemus is very direct. It is clear that he is quite convinced. He says, "Rabbi, we know you are a teacher who has come from God. For no one could do the miraculous signs you are doing if God were not with him."

It is then that Jesus says something that blows Nicodemus' mind. "I tell you the truth, no one can see the kingdom of God unless he is born again." Now we in this day have heard that phrase a hundred times, but Nicodemus is hearing it for the first time. His basic response is, "So somehow at this age I am supposed to end up back inside my mom and be reborn?" He just doesn't get it.

Yet the answer is right in front of him. In order for him to become a follower of Jesus, he would have to give up everything he had ever worked for, basically his whole life. He would have to surrender his whole life in exchange for his faith in Jesus. He would have to die to himself and be what...? You guessed it...he would have to be born again. He would have to start his whole life over. To reap the eternal reward of Heaven, Nicodemus would have to give up all his plans, dreams and ambitions and trust Jesus' plan to be better.

Jesus continues his explanation. "I tell you the truth, no one can enter the kingdom of God unless he is born of water and the Spirit. Flesh gives birth to flesh and the spirit gives birth to spirit." You see being born from his mother is not enough, he must also be born of the Spirit, which happens through Christ. Accepting Christ is the key to salvation and eternal life because it is through the acceptance of Christ, that we receive the Holy Spirit. It is when we receive the Holy Spirit that we are born again.

Nicodemus is still not quite understanding the concept. His head is probably swimming in all the things that Jesus has told him. In fairness, this is a lot to take in for a man who has lived under a different teaching his whole life. We know he must have been very knowledgeable because Jesus refers to him as Israel's teacher. But clearly all Nicodemus' knowledge was not enough. Nicodemus needed the personal relationship with God that comes from knowing Jesus. Nicodemus needed to be born again. Jesus basically asks him if he can't grasp the earthly things how can he possibly expect to understand the things of heaven?

Jesus uses the story of Moses raising the bronze serpent in the desert to explain how he himself must be crucified and "lifted up." Once again, in this we see Jesus giving an example from a perspective that Nicodemus could understand. That is crucial for us to remember as we share our faith. If we speak "Christianese" and give people a whole bunch of terms they can't understand, how can we convince them of their need for Jesus? Nicodemus as a teacher of the law, would have been very familiar with this story and so it was an excellent example to use to help him understand being born again.

In the story the Israelites had once again turned against God and God had enough of them. He sent poisonous snakes among them to bite them and many of the Israelites died. They repented and went to Moses, who prayed for them. God instructed Moses to make a bronze snake and put it on a pole. Anyone who was bitten by a snake could look at the bronze serpent and live. This symbol is still used today by people in the healing professions. Just as the Israelite could look at the bronze serpent and live when they were bitten by the snake so can men and women who are bitten by sin be healed by looking up to Jesus who was lifted up to save us.

Then Jesus gives Nicodemus the most famous verse in all of scripture, John 3:16. "For God so loved the world that he gave is one and only son, that whoever believes in Him shall not perish but have eternal life." It is clear through this verse that the way to heaven and the only way is to accept Christ and the salvation he offers. So, did Nicodemus accept Christ? We don't know for sure, but the evidence is pretty strong that he did. Nicodemus spoke up for Jesus when the Sanhedrin (The ruling body of the Pharisees) was plotting against him. He also joined Joseph of Arimathea in claiming the body of Jesus and purchased the spices for his burial. Keep in mind this was when most of Jesus disciples were in hiding and fearing for their lives. It would seem that not only did he become a believer, Nicodemus was growing in his faith. One thing is for certain though, Nicodemus was no longer sneaking around in the dark. He was out in the open about his relationship with Christ and if you ask me, that is Radically Real!

Chapter 4

A Free Gift

That Will Cost You

Everything

Radically Real Service and Obedience

Therefore I urge you, brothers in view of God's mercy, to offer your bodies as living sacrifices, holy and pleasing to God--This is your spiritual act of worship. Do not conform any longer to the pattern of this world, but be transformed by the renewing of your mind. Then you will be able to test and approve what God's will is his good pleasing and perfect will.

--Romans 12: 1, 2 (NIV)

Living Sacrifice, What Does That Mean?

Make yourself a living sacrifice...huh? The statement conjures a whole bunch of images of martyrs from long ago. Joan of Arc being burned alive, missionaries boiling in the giant pots of cannibalistic tribes and of course Jesus, suffering and dying for our sins on the old rugged cross come to mind. Of course, that is the supreme sacrifice and thousands of people have given their lives to spread the Gospel between Jesus and today. Being a living sacrifice, goes far beyond that however. Being a living sacrifice means that everything you have and everything you do and everything you are is on the altar at the full disposal of God.

We sing songs in church like "Where He Leads, I'll Follow" all the time. But do we ever consider what that means. It means if God calls us, we are willing to lay aside our plans to do His will. That means when we see a need we go out of our way to meet it in the name of Jesus. It may mean going to a far-off land to preach the Gospel. It may mean serving at the homeless shelter or giving money to people who desperately need it. It may mean stopping along the road to help a senior citizen fix a flat tire. It may mean opening up your home to a family that needs your help or simply providing a meal for a family with a new baby or a sick relative. In short it is about service and seeking to do the will of God. When you see a hurting person, that is God calling. When a person has a need and you have what they need, that is God calling. When you see a person in need of help and you have the ability to help, that is God calling. Maybe you are not physically able to help that person with the flat tire, but you have a cellular phone, to call a tow truck. That means God has given you the resources to help that person. Radically Real Christians do not ignore a neighbor in need. Radically Real Christians are always ready to lend a helping hand. Are you ready?

Jesus modeled this for us in John 13. The disciples were in the upper room and Jesus, the Son of God, took off his cloak, put a towel around his waist and began to wash their feet. Jesus was showing us something important in this example. There he was, King of Kings and Lord of Lords doing the work of a lowly house slave. His message was simple. In the world, to be great is to be served by everyone else. To be great in the kingdom of God you must be willing to be a servant. Service can be as simple as offering a cup of cold water to someone who is thirsty, or being a shoulder to cry on, or simply providing a listening ear--or it can be as complicated as serving in the mission field in some far-off country.

There is one thing unique to being a Christian servant though, and that is this, Christian servants are always quick to pass the glory for their service onto Christ. The Bible says "some live their lives as unto men and they have their reward." If you serve for your own personal glory, to gain status, the status is your reward. Christian servants serve to the glory of God. As Jesus says in Matthew 5:16, "Let your light shine before men that they might see your good deeds and praise your Father in Heaven." Whatever we do should be done to God's glory, out of love for him and out of gratitude for the gift of salvation. Salvation was given freely, and when we accept Christ, we are given it free of charge. But in gratitude, we must be willing to give all we have to God.

The truth of the matter is that when we accept Christ, we accept God and we accept Him for who He is: the creator of all things, the sustainer of life, the maker of the universe. If we accept this we must come to an unavoidable conclusion. Everything belongs to Him. Everything we have is a gift from Him to be used for the good of His Kingdom. From our material possessions, to our talents to our very lives, it all belongs to Him. When we reach this conclusion, we cannot help but serve him, and since he gives us everything we need to serve Him we should not be able to serve Him without giving Him the glory.

So, where are all the servants? If you regularly attend church, you know where I am going with this. At my church I call them "the usual suspects". They are the ones that show up early to every function and are the last ones to leave. They are deacons, Sunday school teachers, board members, and more. If there is anything to be done you can be sure they will be there. These people have the service thing down to a "t". If you don't know who they are, you're probably not one of them or perhaps your church has mastered the even distribution of the work (if you are in the latter group, fall to your knees right now and praise the Lord.) If you are not serving, pray and ask God how you can best be used, go to your pastor and tell him you want to serve and then get to work. We always run the risk of burning out "the usual suspects." If even one of them leaves, you will probably need to fill six or seven jobs. Wouldn't it be better to jump in and lighten their load a little? Make no mistake about it, everyone is called to serve, and the more that are serving the more that can be done, the more that can be done the better the church will be. The better the church is the more people will come and the more people that come, the more people you can reach for Christ, which is the real purpose of the church.

Each person is gifted differently, but everyone has a gift. Not everyone can preach from the pulpit, but everyone should be able to tell someone, one on one, about his or her faith. Some people have a gift of service or a gift of hospitality, let him or her serve in your meals or help in a ministry to a homeless shelter. Somebody may be very mechanical, let him or her help work on the building. Church buildings always seem to need some kind of maintenance. There might be someone in your congregation that has an ability that is not currently being used in any ministry of your church. Create one for them, get everyone involved.

There is one other thing to consider. Don't expect everyone to be good at everything. When I first joined my church, they made me a trustee. In our church, the trustees do of a lot of the work on our 150-year-old building. I have no mechanical ability whatsoever and people just assumed that because I was young and male that I could just automatically fill in, pick up a hammer and get to work. It was one of the most frustrating experiences of my life. I desperately wanted to help but when I got with all the mechanical guys, I hadn't a clue what I was doing. I felt extremely useless. It was embarrassing to be so incompetent. What finally happened is I discovered that I was able to serve by doing the non-mechanical things, "the grunt work," and letting the experts do their thing. It was a way to serve and I will still do this type of thing when the trustees need help, but being a trustee was not the best way to use my abilities. It was very unfulfilling.

Then the pastor found out I had art talent. He asked me if I would paint the backdrops for the Vacation Bible School. I was in my element then, I was using my gift for the Kingdom, it turned out great, I was happy, the church was happy and everyone enjoyed it and came away blessed. I have done the backdrop every year since, although these days, I use it as a youth group activity, allowing talented kids to use their talents for the kingdom too. Being involved in the backdrop got me interested in the Vacation Bible School, and one year when they had a teaching vacancy, I took the job and had a great time. Then someone asked me if I would like to participate as an actor in the skits. This was a challenge for me, I was a person who was very shy to be in front of a crowd speaking, but since our VBS is primarily children, I decided to tough it out and give it a try. I had a great time and discovered a new way to serve in my church. I will never win an Oscar, but I like to act and would participate in skits and other illustrative dramas. This gave me confidence to speak in front of the congregation. Now, with the call to the ministry, I have the ability to stand in the pulpit with confidence.

God had his hand in this and was preparing me for my calling, but the pastor taking the time to identify my most basic gift helped to get me to this point. Challenging people is OK. It is in fact how they grow, but start off where they are gifted and let them shine. We all have a place to serve in the Kingdom. By helping people find their place to serve you help them to become Radically Real.

Not My Will...

Jesus was in the garden in Gethsemane. He knew his hour was at hand. He knew His earthly ministry was nearing its end. He knew the pain and agony He was about to suffer and He knew it was coming soon. He went to God. Falling on His face before God, He asked God if there was an alternative to what He was about to suffer. He asked God to take away the "cup" He was about to drink from. He was sweating profusely, the Bible says as drops of blood. And then He said the crucial thing, "but not my will but yours be done." We have salvation because of that line. You see I truly believe that Jesus could have picked up and walked away from it right there. He could have said, "enough of you people, what more can I do for you? I have done amazing things in your sight and still you do not believe." He could have said, "I've had it with you." He could have called down the host of heaven struck down the opposition and set up His own kingdom. He could have, but he didn't. Instead, He did the Will of the father. He went to that cross and let sinful men drive nails through his hands and feet so that the very people that drove the nails might have salvation.

We can learn something from this. The easy thing for Jesus to do for Himself would have condemned us all to Hell. Jesus chose to do the hard thing and a very hard thing it was. Doing God's will for us, meant He was spit on, cursed, beaten, humiliated, stripped, and had large spikes driven through His hands and feet. He was then lifted up to hang from the nails through His flesh. Death by crucifixion is accomplished by suffocation. A person cannot fill their lungs because of the way they are hanging. The Romans had different ways of crucifying. The first was to simply nail the hands above the head. Death came quickly in this way. The way Jesus was crucified was different. People crucified this way were guaranteed a slow painful death. You see, as stated earlier, crucifixion brought death by suffocation but by nailing the feet, a person could push up on the nails through their feet to gain air. Of course this brought agony with every breath. The instinct to survive was in constant battle with the agony. Make no mistake about it, Jesus suffered to do the Will of His Father. Praise God that He decided to do His Father's Will.

Let's bring it home. Are you seeking to do the Father's Will? In order to do the Will of the Father, we must first know what His Will is. Do you ask Him to reveal His Will for you? Do you ask Him to help you to use your talent for His Kingdom? All these things are important. Obviously, you can't do His Will if you don't know what it is. Daily prayer is so important for this purpose. A Radically Real Christian must seek the Will of the Father daily!

The purpose in life of the Radically Real Christian is to bring honor and glory to God. How better can we do this than if we are living out His perfect plan for our lives? The plan that he designed for you, the plan he designed you for. When we are in His Will we are capable of doing amazing things. Does this mean they will be easy? Absolutely not! I believe that trials are strengthening exercises that further prepare us to do the Will of the Father. Believe me, it's much easier to see this from the other side of the trial, but nonetheless, I have found it to be true. Think about all the things Jesus went through to fulfill God's Will.

He was born in a stable. One of the first things that He had to do (with his parents help since He was a very small child) was to flee for his life from Herod. Even though we don't know much about his childhood, we can nevertheless, in seeing the way well-behaved children are treated by their peers, make the assumption that Jesus' childhood may not have been easy as the perfect, sinless, Son of God. When He grew up, as God incarnate one might assume that He would have set up operations in a fancy house and let the people come to Him. Of course, that assumption was wrong. No fancy house, no big church with the self-portrait stained-glass windows for Jesus. No, Jesus was the prototype for Radically Real Christians. He took it to the streets. He reached out to the people that the religious leaders would not have touched with a ten-foot pole. This caused the "respectable" people of the day to look down on Him, but make no mistake about it, it was the Will of the Father.

Jesus then went on a forty day fast, not in a comfortable bed but in a hot steamy desert. Why? For the express purpose of being tempted by the devil. You think you face temptation? One can imagine that Satan threw everything that he had at the Son of God. After all, what greater prize for the one who sought to assume the throne of God than to corrupt and turn His Son? Why do you think that God allowed Jesus to suffer in this way? I believe the answer is to prepare Him for the ultimate test. The temptation to leave the cross behind, to wipe us out and start over, to call down those angels, to avoid that pain and leave us all to struggle and earn our own salvation and to be great in the eyes of the world. After all it is not like Jesus ever received the respect he deserved.

Even today men disrespect Him and His children on a daily basis. And yet, Jesus paid it all. Why? Because in the end, His love for us and His obedience caused Him to do the Will of the Father. In spite of all the persecution, doing the Will of the Father was His ultimate goal. It was God's plan for His life, and He saw it through to the end. As a result, God's ultimate victory was completed and we get to reap the benefit.

To be Radically Real in the pursuit of God's will, is to keep your eyes on the prize. To realize that God's plan is perfect and that He will never let you down. It is the realization that trials will come, and the acceptance of God's promise to be with you through it. Hold fast to Him and He will bring you success if you are in line with His will. What a great reason to be Radically Real in your pursuit of God's Will.

Counting the Cost

Jesus said that whoever wants to be His disciple, must count the cost and take up his cross daily and follow Him. If you really want to be a disciple of Jesus, it will cost you something.

This is different from earning Salvation. Salvation is free, bought by Jesus blood on the cross. By accepting Him and repentance from your sin you will go to Heaven. But there is more. Being a Radically Real Christian means more than just accepting Christ. It means that you desperately want to serve Him and share Him with all the people God gives you. It means that above all else you want to be His disciple, to do the Will of the Father and to always be ready to share the reason for your hope in Jesus. To be His disciple can be costly and Jesus is telling us to make sure we are up to the challenge.

Here is the bad news. You are not up to the challenge. On your own, Satan will eat you alive. No, you have to be careful to make sure that as you step up to the plate to be a Radically Real disciple of Christ that you are always with the Lord. You have to know that your only hope of success is found in your relationship to Jesus. You have to stay close to Him. How do you do that? By spending time with Jesus, through prayer and spending time in the Word of God.

What Jesus is saying in telling us to count the cost is that we must be willing to look at the sacrifice that He made. He surrendered comfort in Heaven for the pain of the cross. He is asking us if we are willing to do the same. Are we willing to leave the place where we are comfortable, our comfort zone if you will, and go out into the world and complete the plan He has for us?

There is an old saying. "Obstacles are what we see when we take our eyes off of the goal." Nowhere is this more true than in the life of the Radically Real Christian. As a Christian we are aliens in this world, trying to get home. Heaven is our home. We are here because we have a mission to complete and message to share. You see Heaven is the goal, returning to our Father in Heaven, our mission complete and ready to enter into the reward He offers. God needs to be the focus of the life of a Radically Real Christian. We need to keep our eyes on Him if we want to complete our mission. If we look away from the goal, we start to see all the obstacles that are before us, the stumbling blocks that the devil puts in our way. When we look down, away from God, we start to look at these huge obstacles and try to figure out how we can surmount them in our own power, rather than looking to the goal and realizing that it is the power of God guiding us through.

If the obstacles in your life are looking too big right now, I have some good news for you, you're right. The obstacles are too big for you and you are too weak to complete your mission. (Dave, I thought you said this was good news!) Be of good cheer, it is good news. There are two verses from the Bible that break it down. The first is 2 Corinthians 12:9, "My grace is sufficient for you for my power is made perfect in weakness (NIV)." Make sure that you read that right. His power is made perfect in OUR weakness, not His. What God is saying is this, His strength is revealed in our weakness. When you get through a situation that you know was way over your head, don't pat yourself on the back--fall to your knees and look to Him. He brought you through. The second verse gives me more hope than almost any other in all of the scriptures, "I can do everything through Him who gives me strength (NIV)." There is nothing I cannot do when I tap into the strength of almighty God.

As we count the cost of living for Jesus, as we count the cost of being a Radically Real Christian, it should be abundantly clear that the cost of following the Lord is the best investment we can make. It allows us to reap eternal dividends. As a living sacrifice, as a Radically Real Christian, we give up a life we cannot keep to gain a life we cannot lose.

Radically Real People from God's Word

Paul and Ananias

Looking at the life of the Apostle Paul, at first it is hard to see how he ended up where he did. This proud young Pharisee really seemed to be on the fast track. No Pharisee was more zealous. He saw this new movement of followers of Jesus as an uprising that quickly needed to be nipped in the bud. He supervised the slaying of Stephen for example, and he had just gotten permission to round up the followers of Jesus in Damascus for imprisonment and punishment and death. But of course, he never completed that mission. On the road to Damascus, something happened that would change Paul's life forever.

Paul had a one-on-one encounter with Jesus and after that Paul would never be the same again. Paul was walking on the road when a blinding light blocked his path and Paul (who at that time still went by the name of Saul) fell to his knees. He heard the voice of Jesus saying, "Saul why are you persecuting me?"

Can you imagine the fear that Paul was experiencing at that moment? Jesus said, "It's me that you're persecuting, Jesus Christ now get up and go to the city and do what I tell you." Paul's reaction to this is something we cannot afford to miss. Paul was struck blind by Jesus' light, but he didn't say, "I can't go, I can't see." He also didn't second-guess himself and say, "That couldn't have really been God back there or He wouldn't have struck me blind." He got up and with the help of the men with him, he went to Damascus.

In Damascus, we find the second Radically Real person in our story, Ananias. Ananias was a just a Christian minding his own business, when God came to him in a vision. God told him to go to the house of Judas on Straight Street and there he would find Saul of Tarsus, who was blinded. God told Ananias to lay his hands on Saul and restore his sight. A light bulb goes off in Ananias' head and he says something to the effect of, "Whoa God, Saul of Tarsus is a bad dude. Soon after I lay my hands on him, what's to keep him from laying his hands on me and taking me back to Jerusalem?" God told him that Saul was his chosen person to go and take the message of salvation to the Gentile world. Ananias immediately trusted God and went to Saul, and when he touched Saul, the scales fell off of his eyes and Saul saw the light.

From that day forward, Saul who was now Paul, never turned back. He founded many churches and he endured much persecution. He was imprisoned, shipwrecked, beaten and finally killed for the message He gave his life to spreading. In the early days, one can imagine, he faced resistance and distrust from all sides. Some of the Christians had to be concerned that all this was a trap. Paul had to convince them not only of his message, but also his sincerity.

There are many things that can be learned from Paul and Ananias. From Ananias, we can see that it is always important to trust God, and that God is always trustworthy. When Ananias first heard he was to go to see Saul, he was hesitant. In truth, why would anyone not be? Saul was after all, a reputed persecutor of Christians. It was clear that Ananias already knew of Saul's original plan for the Christians in Damascus and yet when God told him what to do, Ananias put it all on the line to follow God, trust in Him and do His will. That is the kind of faith Radically Real Christians must possess.

From Saul, a few things come to mind. The first is "Why Saul?" Surely God could have found someone that would have been a lot easier to trust for the early church than Saul. I mean after all, Saul was a big-time persecutor of Christians. Saul put fear into a lot of the early church and now God was using him to share the Gospel. The answer is simple really, Saul was ultimately dedicated to God. Even in his persecution of the early church, Saul was acting out of dedication to God the Father. Saul was defending his faith. To reach Saul, God simply had to show him that Jesus was the Messiah and He knew that Saul would lay down his life to spread the Good News. God can use anyone. God works in the lives of some of the most unlikely people and uses them to serve His Kingdom. As we look at the life that Paul lived one thing is clear, Paul was one of the most Radically Real Christians that ever lived and God, as usual, knew exactly what He was doing.

Paul counted the cost, he put his life as a Pharisee behind him and focused his sights on God. He trusted that God's plan for his life would be the best plan there was. It was through that plan for Paul that many of us of the Gentile persuasion are Christians today. Paul (through the inspiration of the Holy Spirit) was the writer of over half of the New Testament. Through all the persecution he endured, God was faithful to Paul and Paul was faithful to God and that in the end is the best example there is of being Radically Real.

Chapter 5

Love Is The Key

Radically Real Love

And now I will show you the most excellent way. If I speak in the tongues of men and of angels, but have not love I am only a resounding gong or a clanging cymbal. If I have the gift of prophecy and can fathom all mysteries and all knowledge, and if I have faith that can move mountains, but have not love, I am nothing. If I give all I possess to the poor and surrender my body to the flames, but have not love, I gain nothing.

Love is patient, love is kind. It does not envy, it does not boast, it is not proud, it is not rude, it is not self-seeking, it is not easily angered, it keeps no record of wrongs. Love does not delight in evil, but rejoices in the truth. It always protects, always trusts, always hopes, always perseveres.

Love never fails, but where there are prophecies, they will cease; where there are tongues, they will be stilled; where there is knowledge, it will pass away. For we know in part and we prophesy in part, but when perfection comes the imperfect disappears. When I was a child, I talked like a child, I thought like a child, I reasoned like a child. When I became a man, I put childish ways behind me, now I see a poor reflection as in a mirror; then we shall see face to face. Now I know in part; then I shall know fully even as I am fully known.

And now these three remain: faith hope and love. But the greatest of these is love.

--1 Corinthians 13(NIV)

The greatest of these is love...Greater than hope...Greater than faith...Why? Very simply put, God is love and God is greater than all else. Ask a person to define love and they are likely to stumble with the term. They may describe a feeling, though this is usually more like infatuation than real love.

They may speak of love at first sight. To my mind this is nearly impossible. The fact of the matter is that love has very little to do with sight and first impressions. Surely the romantic love most people think of when they think of love, usually starts off as infatuation but in order to last for the long-haul people must get far beyond infatuation. Some people speak of making love. Personally, I think this term should be stricken from the English language. Sex can no more make love than monkeys on typewriters can write the words of Shakespeare. How many lives have been ruined by as a result of people giving their bodies in exchange for the hope of love? How many people have created for themselves a life of pain by seeking love through sex. Love will never, ever come from sex.

Love is not just a feeling. As dcTalk would say, "love is a verb". Love is something you do. Love is giving of yourself. Love is the act of caring for someone whether or not they care for you, it is selfless, and unconditional. If you are looking for what you can get out of it, it is not really love. It is what you give in love that counts.

The love of God is like that. We have nothing that God needs. There is nothing He can gain by loving us and yet He does. In fact, not only can He not gain from us, but He has to give us everything that we need, right down to the air we breathe. His love is truly unconditional. He cares for us no matter what we do. Even when we turn against Him, He is ready willing and able to forgive us and take us in and restore us to our position if all we will do is turn from our ways and return to Him. His love is ultimately sacrificial. He was willing to give His only son, to allow Him to die a horrible painful death so that any lowly sinner, any criminal, thief or murderer, can turn from his sin, turn to Him, believe and be saved. One thing is clear, the Bible says that God is love at least partly to show that when God says to love thy neighbor, He expects us to follow his example and not just apply lip service to the principle.

Faith, hope and love remain and the greatest of these is love. Notice the importance of love. The Bible tells us that faith is what saves us, and yet we see here that love is greater. I have wondered about this and have come to this conclusion: love is the sign of our faith. If we have faith in God, then we will love our neighbor.

Love... The True Mark of a Believer

Look at what Jesus says, "By this all men will know that you are my disciples, if you love one another" (John 13:35 NIV). In this verse, Jesus makes it very clear that if we are to follow Him, we must love one another. Hate has no place in the life of the Radically Real Christian. Over the years, many people have twisted the words of scripture to support a myriad of beliefs and hateful practices, from the slavery in the pre-civil war south, to racism, to spousal abuse, to genocide. In this verse Jesus smashes all those twisted conclusions and makes one thing abundantly clear, the mark of a true Christian is his love for his fellow man.

Still not convinced? Then check out this passage from 1 John: "We love because He first loved us. If anyone says, "I love God," yet hates his brother, he is a liar. For anyone who does not love his brother, whom he has seen, cannot love God whom he has not seen. And He has given us this command: whoever loves God must also love his brother." (1 John 4:19-21 NIV)

The reason to love is because God loves you. Think about that for a minute. God, the creator and master of all there is loves you, warts and all, no matter what the sin that might separate you from Him. No matter what you have done, God loves you. Pretty cool, huh. You are loved by the Creator of the universe. That's enough to give anyone a happy chill. But check it out, if you say you love God, but hate your brother, (or anyone else) you are a liar. The proof that you love God is in how you treat other people. More specifically, the proof that the love of God is in your life is the way you treat others. Why? It's very simple really. If you can't love the person you can see, the person God has put in your life to minister to, how can you love God whom you can't see? Put another way, every man, woman and child on the face of the earth is a person loved by God. If we love Him, should we not love those that He loves? Now rest assured, I believe that God knows that this is not always easy, but also rest assured that you are not always easy to love either and yet God loves you. It is clear from the word of God that if we love Him we will find a way to love even the most un-loveable. The closer you can get to this, the closer you are to being a Radically Real believer.

Let's examine another passage from 1 John. Actually, this passage precedes the one we just looked at: "God is love. Whoever lives in love lives in God, and God in Him. In this way love is made complete among us so that we will have confidence on the day of judgment, because in this world we are like Him. There is no fear in love. But perfect love drives out fear. The one who has fear is not made perfect in love." (1 John 4:16b-18 NIV)

God himself is love; the spirit of love is the spirit of God. We are commanded to follow the example of God; shouldn't we also be walking examples of love. The Radically Real Christian is one that shows loving kindness to everyone we meet. We need to show that love by being there for people when we are needed, helping when help is needed, supporting when support is needed and loving when love is needed. The very act of living in God, of having God in our lives means we must live a life of love.

Look at what it says next, "In this way love is made complete among us so that we will have confidence on the day of judgment". What does this mean? The love in our lives is the evidence of God in our lives, and God in our lives through the salvation in Jesus Christ, is what we need on the day of judgment. You see love is not a matter of life and death, it's so much more important than that. Love in your life, love for others is the sign that you have salvation. When we love we are like God. That's pretty cool, isn't it?

"There is no fear in love, but perfect love drives out fear. The one who has fear is not made perfect in love." How can this be? Well, we said before that love is the sign of God in your life, the sign of salvation through the blood of Jesus. When we have salvation, fear loses its strength. Why? When we have salvation, we are promised eternal life in heaven. Faith in God and his promises, lets us know that the very worst thing this world can do to you is send you to heaven faster. The more perfect in love you become, the less fear there will be in your life. Put another way, when we fear, we are not putting our full faith in God. As we mature in our faith, as we grow more confident in the love of God, which is evident in our love for others, we will feel less and less fear.

Jesus turns it up a notch in Matthew chapter 5: "You have heard it said, 'Love your friend and hate your enemy.' But I tell you Love your enemies and pray for those who persecute you, that you may be sons of your Father in heaven. He causes the sun to rise on the evil and the good and sends rain on the righteous and the unrighteous. If you love those who love you, what reward will you get? Are not even the tax collectors doing that? And if you greet only your brothers, what are you doing more than others? Do not even the Pagans do that much? Be perfect, therefore, as your Father in heaven is perfect." (Matthew 5: 43-48 NIV)

I can just imagine what the people must have thought as they were hearing this part of the Sermon on the Mount. "Love your enemies? Pray for those who persecute you? You have got to be kidding!" No, friends this was no joke. Remember in the last scripture when we read that perfect love drives out fear. Perfect love means love for everyone, even those that would do you harm.

Love is the evidence of God living in us, remember. Our faith in His promises allows us to put fear aside and reach out to those who clearly do not have our best interest at heart. Jesus is calling us to step our faith up to the next level. Of course there is something else to consider. The love of Jesus changes lives. It is an undeniable truth of life. When we reach out in love to someone we perceive as an enemy, we may be doing something for them that has never been done before. Instead of allowing hostilities to escalate, we are showing on our part there is no malice. We are showing love. We are showing that there is a better way. There are thousands of stories of people that have turned an enemy, a persecutor, into a brother or sister in Christ. This is the true goal of every Radically Real Christian.

Jesus modeled this for us perfectly on the cross. He had been beaten and bloodied, He had been spat upon by the very people He came to save, He had nails driven through his hands and feet so that his suffering on the cross would be the most horrible that it could be. He was impaled through the side by a spear. This was the treatment He received for coming so that we might have life and have it more abundantly. Did He call down fire from heaven? Did He call down a legion of angels to destroy them? Did he strike them down with plague or pestilence? Were his persecutors struck down? No! He was capable of that. All those things were at His disposal, but he didn't use them. Instead, He hung there in a pain that we could not bear to imagine, sweat and blood and tears running down his face, gasping for every breath. He said to His Father in Heaven, "Father forgive them for they know not what they do." Now that's a love that is Radically Real.

The Most Important Commandment

Jesus was once asked what is the most important commandment. His answer was this: "Love the Lord your God with all your heart, and with all your soul and with all your mind. This is the first and the greatest commandment. And the second is like it: love your neighbor as yourself. All the law and the prophets hang on these two commandments." (Matthew 22: 37-40 NIV)

Love for God is the most important love there is. If you love anything in your life more than God, put it on a shelf and bow down to it, because it is your "god." This will probably not be the last time you see this quote in this book, because it is one of the most important concepts for the church today. The first commandment tells us that we shall have no other gods before God. God demands our love and He demands to be first in our lives and he is worthy. He has given us life and all we have, from the air we breathe to the home we live in, to our families, to our material blessings. He is worthy of all our praise.

In today's society we have made as many "gods" as any pagan society in the past. We have a false sense of security because we aren't bowing down to a statue of it, but make no mistake about it, if it comes before God, it is an idol. (See chapter 10 for more on this subject). Putting God first in your life is the surest way to make sure the rest of your life is in order.

The second most important commandment is also very interesting. Notice that Jesus puts it almost on the same level as the first commandment. Love your neighbor as yourself. In our society today, "looking out for number one" is a way of life. In the relentless pursuit of self- gratification, too often we forget about the people that are affected by our actions.

Companies in pursuit of the almighty dollar will devastate whole communities by pulling their operations out of a community to save on taxes and wages. The very people that made them wealthy are forgotten in exchange for the almighty dollar. Union negotiators will price those same people out of jobs rather than make a mutually beneficial compromise. Unless "looking out for number one" means seeking to do the Will of God and serving His children, it is a recipe for disaster. The plan Jesus commands is that we look out for each other, that we help each other out, that we keep each other's best interests at heart. Can you imagine how that world would look? Can you imagine a world where people made decisions based on the golden rule? Do unto others as you would have them do unto you--has become, do unto others then leave before they catch you. Radically Real Christians make their decisions with prayer and consideration for how their actions will affect not only their lives but also the lives of others.

Jesus then says that these two commandments cover all the law and the prophets. This is true and can be seen by looking at any commandment. "Thou shalt not kill," would you kill someone that you love as much as yourself? "Honor you father and mother," would you honor your parents or anyone for that matter that you love as much as yourself? "Thou shalt not steal," would you steal from someone you love as much as yourself ? The list goes on and on. The strongest our society could ever be is if God is first in our society and if the people are looking out for each other. This is a challenge to Radically Real Christians everywhere, to model a life that puts God first and looks out for others. If you are this kind of Christian, you will be a shining example in a dark world and people will be drawn to you.

No Greater Love

Jesus said, "greater love has no man than this that he lay down his life for his friends." (John 15: 13 NIV). Jesus, of course, modeled this like no other, in his sacrifice on the cross for all of us. Even though we were sinful and unworthy, Jesus in His love gave His life for us. This was the supreme act of love. There have been many people that have given their lives and been martyred for their love of God. From Stephen on, Christians have often paid the supreme sacrifice rather than deny their faith.

Giving our lives for our friends does not necessarily mean that the person will have to experience physical death however. A person can lay down their life as living sacrifice. A life of unselfish giving to all who are in need is a prime example. Laying down your life for a friend might mean to miss your planned dinner to help a stranger change a tire. Laying down your life might mean taking your time to work in a ministry. Giving your life to a bunch of kids, sharing the Gospel with them, taking them places, being a father to the fatherless, a mother to the motherless, a friend to the friendless. Giving your life might mean serving in a homeless shelter or sharing a smile with a sick person in a hospital. It might be visiting a "shut-in" or just giving a cup of cold water. Love manifests itself in many different ways, but one thing must be for certain. When we serve as an act of love, Radically Real Christians must be sure that we serve in the name of Jesus. If we let people believe that we are serving just because we are good people, we do not point them to the Lord. We simply glorify ourselves and not the Lord and Radically Real Christians live to glorify the Lord. So how about you? Are you laying down your life for others? To be perfected in our love, it is clear that we must love sacrificially.

Who Is My Neighbor?

No, it is not just the person next door. Your neighbor can be anyone, or more specifically your neighbor could be everyone. Being instructed to love your neighbor basically means that you must show love to all you come in contact with. As a Radically Real Christian, God has assigned you a mission, a mission to reach out to people with the Gospel, to share the love of Jesus and to go into the world to make disciples. Quick review...How will people know that we are Jesus disciples? That's right, by the way we love one another. So if we are to make disciples of the people God puts into our lives, Radically Real Christians must model the love of Christ to all we come in contact with to prepare them to do the same. The people that God puts into your life are the first mission field that God has assigned you to. It is your job through the power of Jesus to reach out to them and shine with his love. If you want to be a Radically Real Christian, Love is the key.

Radically Real Love in the Bible

1 Corinthians 13

Rather than look at a person for our biblical example, I thought we would look at love itself, and what better place to look than at the "love chapter", 1 Corinthians 13. First Corinthians was written by the apostle Paul. It was a letter to the church Paul founded in Corinth.

Corinth was an important trade city in Greece at the time Paul went there. It was a very prosperous place with all the attractions the world had to offer at that time. It was a heavily populated area with as many as half a million people at the time of Paul's arrival. The city was a melting pot of people and cultures. With the vast diversity, cultures and values, the church in Corinth had its share of struggles in living together in unity. Prostitution and immorality were a plague on Corinth by the time Paul had arrived. Pagan worship was everywhere. In short, Corinth was a tough place to be a new believer and it was really a difficult place to start a new church. In another way though, does Corinth really look all that different from modern day America or any other prosperous nation on the face of the earth?

The church in Corinth was falling apart without the presence of Paul. You see Paul moved on onto his next missionary journey and the young church was quickly falling back into the ways of the world. First Corinthians is a challenge to the young church to get back on track.

As we "zero-in" on chapter 13 it is interesting to see where it fits in. It is placed directly between two chapters on spiritual gifts. The beginning portions of chapter 13 lead us to wonder if part of Paul's reason for doing this is because the Corinthians were playing the "I'm holier than you" game. The first three verses of the chapter speak of how the spiritual gifts and even the act of being a martyr are meaningless without love. Paul was warning against going through the motions. He was telling us something very important and it is a message the Radically Real Christian cannot afford to miss. Simply put, whatever you do as a Christian must be done with love. The Bible tells us to speak the truth in love. Too often we speak the truth in pride. We take the "holier than thou" approach which does not reflect well on ourselves or our Savior. That approach does not make people want the salvation that comes from knowing Jesus. Be clear on this, I am not saying to sugar coat the truth or pad it or anything else. Truth is truth. But what I am saying is that we need to have the right attitude, a loving attitude when we speak the truth. Remember, we serve a God who always spoke the truth. He also reached out in love to the very people that society rejected.

Think about the way he spoke to the woman at the well. When Jesus told her she had had five husbands and the man she was living with now was not her husband, he did not say "you filthy harlot, turn or burn!!!" He offered her the living water of His salvation. I think too often, when we deal with others, first we need to take ourselves off the pedestal and realize we are all sinners. We cannot afford to be on a pedestal, because Jesus never put Himself on one. Instead, when Jesus rose above us, it was not on a pedestal, it was on a cross as a sacrifice for all those sinners that He loved so much. Radically Real Christians must carry that same attitude.

Verses four to seven give us the characteristics of love. "Love is patient." Ah, patience the most elusive of all qualities. How often we grow impatient with the people around us. Those very people that Jesus called us to love as we love ourselves, drive us crazy sometimes. Nonetheless, thank God that He doesn't lose patience with you! Every sinful thought we have, every sinful thing that we do grieves the heart of God, yet He perseveres. Shouldn't we? An interesting thing to do with this passage is to fill in "God" in place of the word "love." After all, we read in the scriptures that God is love. When we do that, we see that God is patient. As people who seek to be imitators of God, should Radically Real Christians be any less patient?

"Love is Kind." To see the kindness of God we need look no further than the most famous verse in all of scripture John 3:16. The ultimate act of kindness and love was the sacrifice of Jesus on that cross. The fact that we don't have to go to Hell even though we are worthy of it in our sin and the extravagant gift God gave us in Jesus, and his sacrifice and resurrection show us the kindness of God. God is kind.

"It does not envy, it does not boast." How can we, as Radically Real Christians envy anyone, when we have an amazing store of treasures stored up in our home in Heaven? The fact of the matter is that we are so blessed by our father that we should not have time to envy anyone else. As we look at the blessings of others, we need to see that they are blessings God has given them to fulfill God's purpose for their lives. Rest assured that God will give you everything you need to fulfill His purpose for you.

Boasting is the other side of envy. As Radically Real Christians the only thing we have the right to boast about is God and the amazing grace he showed in saving sinners like us. All the rest of our lives, from the air we breathe on up, are gifts from God. Radically Real Christians always seek to give God the glory. God does not envy, He does not boast. He does not need to do either one. He is the owner and creator of all things, there is nothing for Him to envy. We are His servants and He has no equal so He has no need to boast.

"It is not proud, it is not rude." Pride is the most destructive force in the universe. (Don't hold anything back, Dave tell us how you really feel!) It is pride that caused Lucifer to fall and become Satan. When Satan offered Eve the fruit in the Garden of Eden, he played upon her pride. He told her that God didn't want her to be as good as Him and that is why God didn't want her to eat of the fruit, and we have been struggling ever since. It was pride that brought sin into the world and sin brought disease, pestilence, hardships and death. God is not proud, even though He has the right to be. He and He alone has that right. Love is also not rude. Will anyone think you love them, that you have a loving attitude if you treat them rudely? Radically Real

Christians must constantly watch their attitude and the way we react to others. God is not rude.

"It is not self-seeking." Selfishness and a loving attitude are mutually exclusive. When we are self-focused it is extremely hard to be loving. When we have a loving attitude, we cannot help but put others first. Radically Real Christians should always be looking out for others. Selfishness has no place in our lives. God is not self-seeking.

"It is not easily angered." Notice first of all it does not say it never gets angry; it just doesn't go off at the drop of a hat. To be loving, Radically Real Christians have to be able to let things go sometimes and not be quick to anger. God is not easily angered. If He was, He would have destroyed the works when the person lifted the hammer to drive the first nail in His hand.

"It keeps no record of wrongs." When we confess our sins, God gets rid of them. He doesn't keep dredging them up. He puts them away farther than the east is from the west. Radically Real Christians have to possess a similar attitude when we forgive each other. Too often we hold on to the wrongs of the past and it clouds our view of the future. God keeps no record of wrongs, neither should we.

"Love does not delight in evil but rejoices in the truth." Radically Real Christians must separate themselves from evil. We must resist temptation. We must stay away from pornography, drunkenness, drugs, fornication and all the other sins that the world tells us are OK. We do not live by the world's standards; we live by God's standards. We must also shine the light of truth. We must always speak the truth in love, but we must always speak the truth. The Bible tells us that the truth will set you free. There is freedom is truth, but you can wind up chained to a lie. God does not delight in evil, because evil brings pain to His heart, but God rejoices in the truth. So should we.

"It always protects, always trusts, always hopes, always perseveres." The love God has for us causes Him to protect us. This is not to say that He doesn't love someone who falls victim to wrongdoing or tragedy. We live in a fallen world where bad things happen that we will never understand this side of the grave. We must also understand that we also experience His protection countless times that we will never know of as well as the times when His protection is obvious. Similarly, we should protect those that we love and we are called to love everyone as God loves us. We need to look out for the interests of others.

Love always trusts. We need to have a trusting spirit. We need to trust in God and we need to trust our fellow brothers and sisters.

Love always hopes. When you have God, you have hope. Peter tells us to always be prepared to give the reason for the hope that you have. Our hope is placed in a God that has no limits. I submit that there is no better hope to have than the hope of eternal life through Jesus Christ.

Love always perseveres. Radically Real Christians are in it for the long haul. We need to tough it out in Christ and persevere to fulfill our mission. We need to stick with that person we witness to that just doesn't seem to get it. We need to stay in the game even though sometimes the odds seem stacked against us. How can we do it when the going gets tough? We need to remember that God always protects, He always trusts, He always hopes and He always perseveres. Last, we need to remember that Love never fails and that means that God never fails. God keeps His promises, God is always there, God will never fail to love you in spite of what you do. God is good.

"Now these three things remain faith, hope and love, but the greatest of these is love." Why? Because God is love. Radically Real Christians can always have faith in Him because of His love. We always may hope because when we hope in God, we hope in the most powerful force that there is. And most importantly we can always depend on God's love!

Chapter 6

The Fight of Your Life

Winning the Battle to be Radically Real

Put on the full armor of God so that you can take your stand against the devil's schemes. For our struggle is not against flesh and blood, but against rulers, against the authorities, against the powers of this dark world and against the spiritual forces of evil in the heavenly realms. Therefore put on the full armor of God, so that when the day of evil comes you may be able to stand your ground, and after you have done everything to stand. Stand firm then, with the belt of truth buckled around your waist, with the breastplate of righteousness in place, and with your feet fitted with readiness that comes from the Gospel of peace. In addition to all this, take up the shield of faith, with which you can extinguish all the flaming arrows of the evil one...Take the helmet of salvation and the sword of the spirit, which is the Word of God.

--Ephesians 6:11-17

Make no mistake about it, this battle will be won or lost on our knees. When you fight Satan alone, you lose! Satan is powerful, it cannot be denied. But there is a common misperception about him. Ask anyone what the opposite of God is and 90% of them will say Satan. That answer is WRONG! Satan is not the opposite of God. Satan is the opposite of Michael or one of the other angels. Satan was an angel created by God to do His work. He was originally called Lucifer. He fell from grace when he got a little "too big for his britches," and tried to take the throne of God. Much like you and me, his pride was his downfall. When he fell, he took one third of the angels with him. These other fallen angels are the demons that torment so many. Hell was created for them not for people, but if we choose to follow Satan, we follow him all the way to Hell.

The good news is that as an angel, Satan's power is limited. He is not all knowing like God is, His power is not as great as God, and He cannot be all places at once like God can. If we look at the book of Job, we see that Satan can do no more than God allows. It may seem that from this all God would have to do is tell Satan no. We may see God as being cruel in allowing this to go on. But that is not how it works. God has given each of us free will. We get to choose whether or not we follow him. We also have him to run to. He has guaranteed to be there for us. Yes, we will suffer. Sin has really messed up this world. The scriptures tell us that rain falls on the just and the unjust, but we can run to God and He will hear our prayers. The reason the world is so hard is because sin is so rampant. Radically Real Christian, never forget where your power lies. Your power lies in the one who overcame the grave. Keep your trust in Him. He is worthy!

You are in the fight of your life. But God did not send you into battle without the proper tools. He gives you armor and a mighty weapon, but you have to put them on! Let's look at the armor of God.

Where's Your Armor?

As we look at the scripture at the beginning of this chapter, we see that God has given us all the armor we will ever need to help us defeat our enemy. Be clear about one thing though, that armor will do you absolutely no good if it is hanging on the hook at home when you need it. You never know when a battle will begin. You have to be ready. You have to put on your armor every day.

The Belt of Truth

The first part of the armor is the belt of truth. That seems to be the thing that holds the whole thing together. The truth of the scriptures can be summed up in one word, Jesus. What does he say in John 14:6? " I am...the truth." Jesus never lied. Every word out of his mouth was true. He can be trusted. The Bible is true, every word of it. When we start to chip away at the truth of God, we begin to chip away at our own armor. We must trust in the Word of God and take Him at His word. You don't believe me? How did Satan first take Eve down? In Genesis chapter three we see Satan say to Eve, basically, "Is that really what God meant?" He got her to question the truth of what God had said and all of mankind fell because of it. God is God and we can trust His Word to be true. The Bible tells us God is not a man that He should lie. His truth holds the whole armor together.

If we look a little farther into this truth, we see that the truth will set us free. The truth of the scriptures frees us to follow Christ without doubt. I maintain that there is more to the truth element of the armor than the truth of the scripture. I also believe that we are affected in our battle by our own regard for the truth. Radically Real Christians always need to be truthful. Lies are a tool of the enemy and they can break down our armor.

If you've ever told a lie, you know how imprisoning they are. You can literally become a slave to a lie. You have to remember everyone you told the lie. You have to remember what the lie was. You have to remember to whom you told what. It goes on and on and on. It robs you of your peace. The truth on the other hand is quite liberating. It remains constant. It is provable. It doesn't matter who you told because it is always right. Further it is the Will of God that we hold on to His truth. His truth is both our hope and our mission.

How can we accomplish our mission of spreading the truth of the Gospel if we get a reputation for lying? Think about someone you know of that has been caught in a lie. Is it easy to believe anything they tell you or are you skeptical of them after a time? As Radically Real Christians we are called to forgive, but aren't we still a bit more cautious about believing someone known to be a liar.

Those people out there in the world are being lied to every day. They are being fed lies from everywhere from Madison Avenue to Washington D.C. Make no mistake about it, no matter where the lies seem to originate, they are just another sin, sent to you courtesy of the father of lies. These lies after a time have hardened many of the hearts of the people you will reach out to. But take heart, what they are looking for is someone who will speak the truth. There is no greater truth that you can share than the truth of the Gospel. This truth holds everything the world is starving for: real honest truth, peace, love and most importantly, hope in a world that has no hope without Jesus. Buckle that belt of truth around your waist and get ready. Now we come to the next part of our armor:

The Breastplate of Righteousness

The first thing I would like you to notice is what the breastplate of righteousness covers. It covers your heart. Your heart is the place where the Lord lives. It is the place that the enemy attacks first. Here is how he does it. He says, "Come on, it's just a little sin, just a little white lie."; "Who's it going to hurt?"; "Go ahead, try it, it'll be fun."; "No one is ever going to know the difference."; "Everyone steals office supplies, it's a big company they owe it to you."; "Nothing is wrong unless you get caught." He gets the ball rolling and once it is rolling it is very hard to stop. It all seems harmless enough, but all sin has a price. Look what the enemy does when you start to witness. "Who are you to tell them about Jesus?"; "Why you are far from perfect."; "Look at all those things you do."; "Look at the way you are living your life."; "You are the last person who needs to be telling people about God, look at you." Even though he was the one who led you down the wrong path in the first place, he uses your sin to convict you and keep you from witnessing. Remember this is the fight of your life you are in.

The answer to the enemy's attacks is simple, righteous living. Now I know what you may be thinking. "It's too late for that I have already lived an unrighteous life." Banish that lie to the pit of Hell where it came from. Of course you have lived an unrighteous life, but remember, "If anyone is in Christ, he is a new creation. The old has gone and the new has come." (2 Corinthians 5:17 NIV)

We have all sinned, but we have forgiveness in Jesus. Any sin can be forgiven. The thing is this, as we are a new creation in Christ, our new goal must be righteousness. We must strive for it every day, we must put on the breastplate and guard our hearts. We must resist temptation. We must realize that every new day is a new battle. We may lose some of those battles but with Christ, we will win the war! When you are tempted to lie, remember the "tangled web" it will lead to. When you are tempted to lust, think about the fact that the person you want to lust after is a child of God, and turn away. When you are tempted to steal (even if it is just a pack of post-its or an extra 15 minutes on your lunch break), think of how you would feel if you lost your most valued possession.

Even better, any time you are tempted to sin, think about the price our Lord paid for your forgiveness. Imagine yourself driving that nail in His hand. Imagine his scream as the iron pierces flesh and guard your heart. Turn away from the temptation. Turn to him. Then thank him for the victory.

Much like the truth, righteousness is also very important to our witness. The world is watching to see what you do. How you live your life is important to your witness. If you tell people about Jesus and then live a sinful life, you are contradicting your own witness. You are also misrepresenting Jesus. People may say, "well if that is what Jesus does in your life, I want no part of Him." We have all sinned, and there are times where we will all fail. This is an undeniable truth. This is an important point. How we deal with our failures is important in how people view Radically Real Christians. It is important that we deal in striving for righteousness and not self-righteousness. All have sinned and fallen short of the glory of God. It is far better to admit your struggle in an area than to try to hide it. Seeing you emerge victorious over a known struggling point will inspire people. Seeing you fall to a hidden temptation will disgust people. I would rather have people see me as a person who is struggling to live a righteous life than for them to see me as a self-righteous person who constantly fails. Self - righteousness is a lie. Our righteousness comes from Jesus.

I think about a man I know. He is not a Christian, but he is someone I care about very much and I very deeply want to see him come to Christ. I pray for him every day. He had a coworker who professed Christianity and then proceeded to live a different way. He would always talk the talk, but he acted worse than the man who is not a Christian. He became very self-righteous with all his co-workers, when he should have been telling them of the one who gives righteousness. My friend came away with the thought, that if I can do better than "Holy Jim" over there what do I need Christ for.

This guy in his actions has turned my friend away from Christ. To this day he is very hard to witness to. Self-righteous Christians turn people away from Christ. Strive for righteousness in Christ and when you fail, confess and try harder in Christ. If you wrong someone ask that person for forgiveness. If a person wrongs you, forgive them.

Radically Real Christian, what do your actions say about your Savior? Put on the breastplate of righteousness. Guard your heart! Then you will be ready for the next part of your armor:

Feet Fitted with Readiness That Comes from the Gospel of Peace

Readiness that comes from the Gospel of Peace...Why is that associated with the feet? I believe it is because we need to go out into the world to share the Gospel. This is "where the rubber meets the road" when it comes to Christian living. You see sharing the Gospel is an active thing. You can't do it just sitting in a pew once a week, you have to be out there, up to your elbows in the world. A vital reminder is necessary here. When you go into the world, remember to be fully armed. Don't forget that breastplate of righteousness.

There are people that I have heard of that will go out drinking to spread the Gospel. If you are even considering such action, forget about it. Remember wherever we go we represent Christ. Yes, Christ did hang out with all kinds of sinners, it's true. However, remember something else, Jesus never sinned. The word of God tells us, "be ye not drunk with wine." If you feel led to witness to people in a bar, make sure you have your armor on. Sinning while witnessing is never a good thing. Some will say "well it is not a sin to drink." But remember what Paul said, referring to certain people eating food offered to idols. "Therefore, let us stop passing judgment on one another. Instead make up your mind not to put any stumbling block or obstacle in your brother's way. As one who is in the Lord Jesus, I am fully convinced that no food is unclean in itself. But if anyone regards something as unclean, then for him it is unclean. If your brother is distressed because of what you eat you are no longer acting in love. Do not by your eating destroy your brother for whom Christ died." (Romans 14: 13-15 NIV) If your actions will cause someone else to sin, your actions are wrong! Radically Real Christians need to remember that our purpose in life is to glorify God.

We must always be ready to share the Gospel, that is why it is part of our armor. It is a state of preparedness that we must always exhibit. We must never allow ourselves to be in a position that does not allow us to spread the Gospel. We must never be seen in public or private in a way that compromises our witness, because we never know when we will be called upon to share the Gospel.

The world is watching. In whatever activity you involve yourself, ask yourself the question, "What if someone needed to hear about Jesus, would I be able to share His love while I am doing this?" A Radically Real Christian is always ready to share the Gospel, 24/7.

The Shield of Faith

Your faith is your shield. It protects you from "the flaming arrows of the evil one." It is your faith in God that brings you through the tough times. It is that faith of knowing that the one who created the universe is capable of caring for us no matter what. Faith is probably the first area where the enemy attacks us, because if he can knock our faith away, we are vulnerable. We need all the power we can get from God to hold on to our faith and fight off these attacks.

The single best attack the enemy has on our faith is when bad things happen to good people. It really makes us shake in our boots when something bad happens to us or to a loved one. We start to look at all the evil people in the world and wonder why us? I remember a time in my life when my grandmother was in the hospital with terminal cancer, suffering in the most horrendous of ways. At the same time one of the serial killers was interviewed on TV in one of those hyped-up specials. I cannot remember which one, and it is really not important for this chapter. What is important is the question I had for God. As I watched, I began to think, "Why does my nana have to die while this evil scourge of humanity gets to live?" I was missing so many things. The first one is this; God loves everyone. The pain my grandmother was in tore at the heart of God, as did all the mental wounds of the killer. Surely the person involved in all this murder and violence, was at some point tortured is some unspeakable way to cause him to do this great evil. Both of these people were suffering but one was close to home.

The second factor to consider is the rain falls on the just and the unjust. One needs look no further than the book of Job to see this played out. The righteous Job had everything. God had blessed him richly for his righteousness. Then one day Satan saw this blessed righteous man and since he hates us all so much, he went to God and said basically, "Oh sure, Job is righteous, but look at all you have done for him. I bet if I attack him and take his blessings away, he'll fall just like all the rest." God allowed Satan to attack Job, and no matter what Satan did, Job did not turn away from God. At one point Job's wife even told him to curse God and die. Things were not going well for Job to say the least. He had lost it all and he did have a lot of questions for God, but in the end he stood strong, and God blessed him even more richly than before. I wanted to bring Job up here to show a few things.

As a new believer, I had a multitude of questions on Job. The first and most obvious was, "is this book for real?" I am not alone in this. The book of Job is somewhat unique in that it gives us a glimpse into the goings on in

Heaven. Some people think this book is a parable. I do not. I think God inspired the writer of the book of Job to write of the events in heaven to show us what happens when bad things happen to good people. I believe that Job is in the Bible to show you and me how to hold on to our faith as the enemy attacks. You see God allowed Satan to attack Job, but he had the breastplate of righteousness on. He also held firm to the shield of faith, even as the enemy did his best to rip it from his hands.

My second major question was simply, "Why?" Why did God allow this? I touched on this a bit in the previous paragraph. Part of the answer is so that we would be able to see that God is in control. Even Satan has to ask permission to do what he does. The other part is this, God, in the book of Job, is showing us that sometimes people's suffering is through no fault of their own. We see this also demonstrated in Jesus and the blind man. Someone asked Him who sinned that the man was blind, was it the man's parents or the man himself? Jesus replied basically neither, that it was so that God could be glorified, and then he proceeded to heal the man. When we stand strong in the Lord, in spite of adversity, He is glorified. God allowed Job to be tormented by Satan so that you and I would be able to see that God is capable of bringing us through anything.

Thirdly, Job shows us who really is to blame for the pain and suffering in the world. It is not God. It is Satan. Sin came into the world and messed up God's perfect creation. Death did not exist before Adam sinned. Sickness did not exist before Adam sinned. Pain did not exist before Adam sinned. Humanity, falling to the temptation of sin is what has caused all these things. (I know some people, especially evolutionists, will want to argue that point. That is another topic for another book, I recommend looking up Ken Ham's *Answers in Genesis* to find out more on the subject.) The fact of the matter is that because people sin, sickness and death come. The Bible says that all have sinned and fallen short of the glory of God. God did not create sin. Sin occurred when man turned from God's way and tried to live on his own terms.

God did, in his infinite love and compassion, give us the way out, in Jesus Christ. It is our hope in Christ that allows us to hold onto our faith. It is Christ that allows us to fight off the flaming arrows of the evil one. The stronger your faith, the bigger your shield.

As Radically Real Christians, we must continually grow in our faith. We must also share our faith and show others how to be protected from the arrows of the evil one. The fact of the matter is that our faith in Christ is what helps us to have hope in the face of adversity. Once you know Jesus and your salvation is secure, you begin to realize that the threats of the world are temporary. Share your faith, Radically Real Christian. Show the world the ultimate shield from enemy attacks.

The Helmet of Salvation

The helmet of salvation, finally you have something to protect your head. The knowledge that you are saved by the blood of the Lamb may be the greatest part of your armor. If God, the creator of the universe is with you, who can stand against you? Wow, talk about comfort. There is such a peace in knowing that the Lord is with you and this is the helmet of salvation. The helmet protects your mind from the attacks that come, because it is these attacks that are some of the most vicious. The thoughts that come into our head can be so destructive. Thoughts of lust, that can be averted when we simply ask ourselves how we can possibly feel that way about another child of God. The constant attacks brought by thoughts of incompetence, unworthiness and on the other end of the scale, pride, that can be averted when we remember the sacrifice Jesus made to save us.

As we put our helmet on, we can begin to see that salvation brings incredible peace. Satan may want to always be reminding you of past sins but the knowledge that you are saved can turn feelings of unworthiness into feelings of great appreciation. Past sin, in the hands of a loving God becomes a powerful testimony to his goodness, mercy and love.

The knowledge of salvation can also work the other way. Knowing you had to be saved shows us the value of our relationship to Jesus. Who can be proud in themselves, when they realize the Son of God had to die for them? This helps us to realize that pride is a useless emotion (except for the pride one can take in Jesus). This allows us to humbly reach out to the hurting. A Radically Real Christian remembers that he is no better and no more valuable than anyone else. He is merely blessed with the free gift of salvation and he has a real duty to share that faith and the hope that comes with it, with a hopeless and hurting world.

The helmet of salvation allows us to know that we can live with confidence, witness with confidence and rest in the fact that Christ has overcome the world. Do you have your helmet on? Do you go to bed at night with the peace of mind of knowing that you have been saved by Jesus' sacrifice on the cross? Are you able to fend off the attacks brought by memories of your past? If not, today is the day to make that change. Today is the day to put on the helmet of salvation. Today is the day to ask Jesus into your heart. Do it! Get your bookmark, put it here and go back to the Salvation prayer found in chapter 3. Pray that prayer! This prayer will help you ask Jesus into your heart and help you on your way to being Radically Real.

The Sword of the Spirit

Finally, we get a weapon. Notice, all the other elements of the full armor of God are defensive. They are made to help and protect. The belt of truth that keeps it all together, the breastplate of righteousness protecting your heart, feet fitted with readiness that helps you move into the world, faith to shield you from the enemy's attacks and finally the helmet of salvation, which protects your head. Now that you are fully armored you are ready to go out.

All that remains is the sword of the spirit, the Word of God. That's right, your weapon in the battle, in the fight of your life is the Word of God, the Bible.

If you are reading this book, it is my hope that your sword is sharp from constant use and not collecting dust on a shelf someplace. If it is, now is another time to get out your bookmark and go dust off your Bible. Reading your Bible is like sharpening your sword. If you are going to survive the battle and win the fight of your life, you have to keep your sword with you at all times and keep it sharp. Am I saying you have to carry your Bible with you at all times? Yes and no. No, in the sense that sometimes you need two hands and you cannot always have your Bible physically with you, yes in the sense that as referred to in the Psalms (119: 11 to be exact). "I have hidden your Word in my heart, that I might not sin against you." (NIV) The key is to keep the Word in your heart even when you can't keep it in your hand.

Psalm 119 is the longest chapter in the Bible, and it is a must read for the Radically Real Christian. It is the instruction manual for your weapon. It tells you how to use it, when to use it and how important it is. It is this simple really, if you are going to win the fight of your life, you need to spend time in God's Word. Read it, study it, live it, learn it, love it. You never know when an attack will come, you have got to be ready. Readiness comes with always being armed with the word.

The enemy knows this. Why do you think it is that the first thing any dictator does is try to remove the church and the Word of God? It is because evil cannot stand against the Word of God. It is truly the world's most powerful weapon. Through the power of the Holy Spirit, it can change evil people to good people. It can change hopeless people into hopeful people. It can and does change lives. In today's church, many people are putting aside the Word of God. They let their pastor teach them once a week, and then they go back out among the "wolves" unarmed and vulnerable to every attack. Don't you dare do that. Every word in the scriptures is worthwhile, valuable and true. You need to be in God's Word daily.

I know that some folks have a bit of difficulty reading the Word of God. They get stuck here and there with something they do not understand and give up or maybe they look at the size of the thing and get intimidated or maybe they think it will be boring. None of these is a really good excuse. If at your job there was something you did not understand, would you give up? Of course not. You'd never be able to hold a job that way. No, you would ask for help or take a course. It is no different with the word of God. First you can ask God for help. Pray before you read and ask God to reveal his truth to you. Next, get involved in a Bible study. Struggle through the tough parts with your brothers and sisters in Christ. If your schedule keeps you from making it to a study, start your own. Get a small group of believers together and study on your own. The other thing is to just take it out and read it. I have read the Bible cover to cover many times and I have to tell you, every time I read it, I find something new. However it works, you have to be in the word of God daily. Satan is a formidable enemy; you have to keep your weapon sharp and ready.

What about the back?

If you have been looking at the full armor of God, you may have noticed that there is nothing to cover the back. What is to keep Satan from attacking you from behind? I thought I would look at two ancient Roman customs as a way of showing how important your back is. The first and most obvious is the *paraclete*. No, a paraclete is not a small bird. That is a parakeet but that is not important now. A paraclete was a partner in battle. Every Roman soldier had a paraclete. In battle, they would link arms and fight back-to-back. Each one would protect the other no matter where the attack came from, one of the soldiers would see it coming and be ready.

Every soldier in the fight of your life needs a good paraclete. You need to have someone who covers your back. This could be your whole congregation, looking out for one another, but preferably in addition to that every Radically Real Believer needs an accountability partner. An accountability partner is someone who will hold your feet to the fire if you need it. He/she is someone who will not think twice about challenging you if you are going down the wrong road. This person will pray for you and you for them. Basically, you have each other's back in the fight of your lives. This person will become your best friend and your strongest ally.

The other Roman tradition is not quite as wholesome. You see a condemned Roman prisoner was sometimes sentenced to death in a unique way. If you were condemned to death, they would sometimes sentence you to live out the remainder of your life with a human corpse tied to your back. Whatever you did, you had to do it with this corpse tied to your back. Eventually the rotting corpse would cause the living person to catch disease and die. This was a slow painful death. As you look for an accountability partner, it is important who you choose. It is important that you choose someone with a faith in God that is growing. That doesn't mean we cannot reach out and help those that are not as far along in their spiritual journey, certainly that is important. But when it comes to an accountability partner, you want someone that will help you fight the spiritual battles and not someone that will cause you to lose faith and die.

Radically Real Christian, you need an accountability relationship to keep you strong in the faith. Find one today. Seek out a friend in the faith, who will be honest with you even if it is painful at times. Take their counsel, pray together and be there for them when they need you. Model Christ for each other. Sometimes they will need to show you great compassion and sometimes they will have to turn over the tables, but in the end, they will help you to be more and more Radically Real.

Don't Leave Home Without Him!

When I was a young adult, not too many years ago, the hottest boxer in the world was Mike Tyson. Mike Tyson's pay-per-view matches were almost a rip-off. He would come out into the ring and within thirty seconds your fifty bucks was gone, the match was over and we were back to regularly scheduled programming. He was an incredible fighting machine. No one would have thought to walk up to him on the street and insult him. And yet every day we come up against a force much more powerful than Mike Tyson and think nothing of fighting him alone. Most of us wear many scars from those battles and yet few of us ever see the light, at least not until we have taken many beatings. I am talking of course about Satan. If we count the Father, Son and Holy Spirit as one (and we should), then Satan is the second most powerful force (though not equal with God) in the universe. How can any of us have the audacity to try to take him alone? We never ever should. We need help and help is readily available.

You see I believe we need to have another look at Jesus and our relationship with Him. Christians are referred to in the Bible as children of God. Jesus is the Son of God. He is in effect our big brother (bear with me here for a second). Satan is the biggest, baddest bully on the block and he is always picking on us. Until one day we get smart. We go walking down the street hand in hand with our big brother, and all of the sudden old Satan ain't lookin' so tough. The key to defeating Satan is Jesus. If we look at Revelation 20:10, we see it clearly. In the end of this mess, Jesus wins. When we stand with Jesus, no one can stand against us, not even Satan. In the Word it says if we resist the devil he must flee. The easiest way to resist the devil is when we are hand in hand with our "big brother." Don't leave home without Him!

Radically Real People from the Bible

Job

Earlier in this chapter we had a look at Job and I thought we would look at his story a bit more in depth here. It was not really easy to pick a person from the Bible to look at for this chapter, because there were so many that truly had to struggle against Satan. Rarely in the Word, however, are we treated to seeing the way Satan will mess with your life as well as in the book of Job.

Job had everything, good family, good health, good home, wealth and in general a good life. And Job was a good man. As a matter of fact, the Bible tells us he was righteous. Satan one day approached God and basically said, "Oh, Job is good all right, but why wouldn't he be, you have given him everything. I bet if you took all that stuff away, he wouldn't be such a goody-goody!" It is at this point that God allows Satan to test Job. Satan systematically takes virtually everything Job has: his wealth, his children even his health. We might say Job is ruined. At one point Job's own wife tells him to "curse God and die." Things are not going well for him, to say the least. It is at this point that Job's "friends" show up. I sometimes wonder if Job's friends were the cause of the old saying, "with friends like these who needs enemies." By the time these three friends (Eliphaz, Bildad and Zophar) show up, Job has been stricken with a painful skin disease. They find him sitting in mourning on an ash heap scraping his sores with a piece of pottery.

Surely you would think that these friends would be there to mourn with him and offer their support. But instead, they begin to lecture Job about what he did to deserve all this misfortune. They believe that what he is going through is a punishment from God. For the Radically Real Christian one of the best things we can do is to read what these three guys did and do the opposite. Pain and suffering are not always punishments from God. Yes sometimes they are the consequences of our actions, but sometimes they have absolutely nothing to do with us. We end up in the wrong place at the wrong time. As Christians, we are not called to act in judgment here. When a person is hurting or in pain, it is our job to help them to find the hope that comes from Christ. If their circumstance is a consequence of their actions, they, on some level, already know it. It is up to us to model the hope shown in Romans 8:28; "In all things, God works for Good of those who love him, who are called according to his purpose." (NIV)

Bad things happen to good people because sin is in the world. God gave us hope of a better day in Jesus. When a person is hurt like Job was, it is our job in Christ to help them stand up again and put their "armor" back on.

In their judgmental attitude, Job's friends put him on the defensive. All of a sudden Job, in addition to all the suffering he is experiencing, now has to defend himself to the ones who came to comfort him. Job has a lot of questions for God. He doesn't understand why he is suffering in this way. Finally, it is time for God to answer Job, and the friends. First of all, God reminds everyone who He is, that He is God and, knowing everything, sometimes things will happen that we cannot understand. It is up to us to believe and have faith that He knows what He is doing. Even when things happen that we cannot understand we must trust God and remember that His ways are beyond our comprehension. Job is humbled; he knows that he must learn to trust God when he can't understand. So must we. We need to be like Job. He wore the breastplate of righteousness, and after the time of testing God blessed him even more richly than before. God returned him to a place of contentment. For a while his shield of faith fell from his hand or at least slipped a bit but in the end God gave a reason to hold tighter to that too.

As Radically Real Christians, we need to trust God at all times, even at the toughest times. We need to hold strong to the shield of faith, especially when we don't understand why things are happening to us. You see, it is at this time when the enemy attacks and tries to turn us from God. We must also be well armed when misfortune comes our way. A Christian's only offensive weapon is the Word of God. The incredible hope we can find in God's Word will help us to fend off the attacks of the enemy. We need to constantly be wearing the breastplate of righteousness, so that we do not fall to the consequences of our own actions. We must hold fast to the belt of the truth, which holds the whole thing together.

When we see others in suffering, we also must also have our feet fitted with readiness to share the Gospel. Job's friends did not do this, they went into being judgmental instead of bringing hope. We must also be sure that we help them to find the helmet of salvation that comes from knowing Jesus.

Radically Real Christians, we are in a war against a very powerful enemy, an enemy who has no purpose but to destroy us. We must remember where our power lies and that "greater is he that is in me than he that is in the world". We must keep fighting the good fight. We must always remember that our first step is always to go with the Master, put on our armor and keep our sword sharp by staying in the Word. The battle is not easy, our enemy is mighty, but in the end, with Jesus, we win!!

Chapter 7

You Can Talk It...
Can You Walk It?

Living a Radically Real Life

You have heard it was said, "Love your neighbor and hate your enemy." But I tell you love your enemies and pray for those who persecute you, that you may be sons of your Father in heaven. He causes the sun to rise on the evil and the good and sends rain on the righteous and the unrighteous. If you love those who love you, what reward will you get? Are not even the tax collectors doing that? And if you greet only your brothers, what are you doing more than others? Do not even pagans do that? Be perfect, therefore as your heavenly Father is perfect.

--Matthew 5:43-48 (NIV)

It's a tall order, isn't it? To be perfect as our Father in Heaven is perfect. And the truth is that it is. He is, after all God. We won't always be perfect, but we should always be striving to do better and better. We should be imitators of God. Our lack of perfection is the reason Jesus had to give His life for us. So why should Jesus tell us to be perfect, when He knows we are not.

Two things come to mind: 1. If we are striving for perfection, we will grow closer and closer to Him in both success and failure and: 2. The people around us expect no less. You don't believe me? What is the first thing the world says when a Christian fails publicly? "...And he calls himself a Christian." The truth is when you claim to be a Christian, people automatically hold us to a much higher standard. Were it not for the grace of God and the leading for the Holy Spirit, the standard would be too high, impossibly high! But we are not alone. We have help. And in Him we can live the kind of life the world cannot argue with.

OK, so you want to be Radically Real. You are seeking God in all you do. You're in the Word. You've got your armor on and then it happens. A temptation springs up out of nowhere. Are you ready? The world is watching.

Jesus tells us to be perfect as He is perfect. He wants us to be strong in Him. He wants us to have a powerful witness to a world that is looking for answers. The world is looking for our hope and it is as if we are in an arena, all eyes are on you. While it may see that the whole world wants you to mess up, to "blow your witness", to be slogging around in the filth with everyone else, the reality is that somewhere deep inside they are pulling for you. Oh it may not seem that way, but we are all children of God and somewhere in our hearts we all want to know He is real and there to help. Some people just hide it real well. The reality is if you are starting to let your light shine, a lot of people will see your hope and want to see you succeed. They want to see a person with peace, hope and joy sticking to their guns and living by their principles. You see they secretly think that if you can do it so can they. They want you to be Radically Real.

You see when Jesus asks us to be perfect as He is perfect, I believe He is giving us a target, a goal, something to shoot for. There is an old saying, "if you aim at failure, you will hit it every time." The saying "nobody's perfect" was blown out of the water on the day that Jesus ascended into Heaven. He made it! Thirty-three years without one moral failure, one impure thought, without spreading one rumor, without falling to one temptation.

I know He was (and is) God, but ask yourself this question. Has anyone in history faced more temptation than Jesus Christ? Jesus made it and in Him we have hope of living the kind of life that will draw others to Him.

Christians, especially Radically Real ones live under a lot of scrutiny. You have got to live your life as if people are watching, because they are. The easiest way to stay on the right path is to live as if God is watching your every move, because He is. Some people get the wrong idea on that, they think that God is watching so He can strike you when you upset Him. We get this picture of God sitting on a cloud with a fresh lightning bolt just waiting for you to mess up. The fact of the matter is that a better image is that we are like toddlers, taking our first steps. Our loving father is behind us every step of the way to steady us and keep us from falling. If we do fall and we reach our hands up to Him, He is there to help us up. He loves you, always remember that.

As you are walking through this world remember the old adage rings true, you are the only Jesus some people will ever see. Truer words were never spoken (except in God's Holy Word of course). When you call yourself a Christian, you become a Christ figure to people. People are looking at you to see what Christ is like (no one said this would be easy). The word "Christian" literally means "Little Christ." How are you doing in representing Jesus?

The Jesus Label...Is He Proud You Wear His Name?

Basically, the answer to that question is yes. He is like a loving father who deep inside is proud of all His kids. He is not cautious with His love either. He loves us lavishly. He heaps his blessings on us over and over again. And yet, I cannot help but wonder if He doesn't wince at times when He watches us in action.

How many times have you seen it happen? Someone tears another person up one side and down the other in the name of Jesus. This is not righteous indignation I am talking about. This is not a "turning over the temple tables" type of rebuke that brings and errant brother or sister back to the straight and narrow. (Sometimes that is called for, but always do it prayerfully.) I am talking about a judgmental "whoopin'" that accomplishes nothing but creating strife, hard feelings and belittlement. Maybe you have been on the receiving end of that or maybe you have done it yourself. I would like to remind those seeking to be Radically Real of Proverbs 15:1, "A gentle answer turns away wrath, but a harsh word stirs up anger." (NIV)

Radically Real Christians need to fight against being judgmental. You can do this by remembering a few things. The first is the verse, "Do not judge or you too will be judged." (Matthew 7:1) Now let me make a statement about that. This statement is a warning about being judgmental from a false sense of superiority. We are all sinners who have fallen short of the glory of God. No one is superior except God. That being said, I want to warn you that that verse has been corrupted, or rather used out of context since the Word of

God is not corruptible, by some people in an attempt to make everything acceptable. There is nothing wrong with using sound judgment. Sin is still (and will always be) sin, and we are called to guard against it.

If these people were to go beyond using Matthew 7:1 as a catch phrase they would see this, "For in the same way you judge others you will be judged, and with the measure you use it will be measured to you." I maintain that the Radically Real Christian's measure should be the Word of God and God's grace. If God says something is wrong, it is wrong. God is the same yesterday, today and forever, and so if that thing we are referring to was wrong, it is wrong and it will remain wrong. We must always remember to show others the grace that has been shown to us. We are not to let everything pass for fear of being deemed judgmental. What we are to remember is that God hates the sin, but loves the sinner. By following God's admonishment to speak the truth in love (Ephesians 4:15), but also standing firm on Biblical principles, Radically Real Christians can be effective in helping people find their way to the straight and narrow.

Another thing we must guard against is adherence to man-made tradition. Now let me state that there is nothing wrong with a godly tradition, but we must be careful. The Pharisees were so blinded by their man-made traditions that they missed out on the Messiah that they had prayed for, for thousands of years. When we chastise and demoralize our brothers and sisters and the rest of the world by heaping requirements on them that are not Biblical, that God never intended, we put up stumbling blocks between people and God. This does not honor Him or help anyone. Make sure that your traditions are Biblical and if they are not, let them go!

Some churches seem to have some sort of unwritten code. They all dress a certain way, act a certain way and have a certain way of doing things and it becomes almost "god-like" to them. To the outsider it looks like they are putting on a show. But they are comfortable going along as they are. Everything is working out fine until one day someone new comes along.

They are not dressed "up to code" or they don't know the traditions or just plain act "different." How do we react to them?

They came in the door seeking God. They came in seeking answers. If they leave having felt nothing but judgment, feeling like an outsider that didn't belong there, have we done our job as faithful followers of God? We are to make them feel welcome. Don't forget what Jesus did. Jesus spent time with what the "respectable" people thought were the dregs of society. He loved them all and so should we! We are supposed to be, in essence, Jesus to them. God will work on the things in their lives that He wants to change. It is our job to love them, accept them, pray for them and show them the way.

When I go to a different church (one other than the one that holds my membership), I can always pick out the Radically Real Christians. They are the ones who go out of their way to greet me and make me feel welcome. Sometimes, they are very boisterous, some are more reserved, but we all should strive to welcome outsiders. Most of the people have no idea who I am. They have no idea about the condition of my spirit. They are merely reaching out to show me the love of Jesus. That is Radically Real and you can bet that if you could see their Father in Heaven, He'd be wearing a big old grin and saying, "That's my Kid!"

A Radically Real Christian lives to glorify God. In other words, we are supposed to be like a child living to make their Father proud. Not long ago I was watching the Olympics on TV and I was struck by something. As the gold medal winner stands on the podium, they always cut to the winner's parents, who are usually crying tears of joy. They are living to see years of their child's work and their own personal sacrifice pay off. Their child has finished well and they have won. One day hopefully, you and I will stand on the podium of Heaven. We will have run the race God put before us and will have finished well and in that moment, we will look to see the face of our Heavenly Father, smiling and saying, "well done, well done!" Radically Real

Christian, that moment will be worth whatever it takes in this life to get there. Run your race well and win! Make your Father proud.

Forgive as forgiven...

We've heard the parable many times in the church, but if you want to read it yourself, you can find it in Matthew 18: 22-35. Peter has just asked Jesus how many times shall he forgive a brother who sins against him. This parable was Jesus' response. Please forgive the paraphrase. A servant owes his master a wad of money, several years' wages in all. His debt comes due and of course, he cannot pay. At this time in history, the master could have had him taken to jail and beaten until he could pay the debt or sold the man and his family to recoup his losses. Instead, he shows mercy and forgives the debt. The servant has been given a fresh start and he is free from his debt.

As he is out on the street celebrating his new found freedom, the servant sees a man who owes him about ten bucks and he flips. The servant grabs the guy by the throat and demands payment immediately. The other man begs for mercy and a little more time to pay, but the servant has him thrown in jail. He seems to have already forgotten the mercy that was shown him that day but the other people on the street have not forgotten it and they go back to the master. When the master finds out he is livid, and has the man brought before him. He tells the servant that he cannot believe after the mercy he had shown that his servant could act this way, reinstates the debt and has the servant imprisoned and beaten until the debt has been paid in full.

This servant is you! The master is God. All Christians have been forgiven a huge debt. Jesus paid that debt himself with his blood, at the price of His own life. How do you attempt to repay His generosity? The debt is your sin. When someone wrongs you, how do you act? Do you forgive as you have been forgiven or do you carry a grudge forever? Jesus told that parable for a reason. The cost of unforgiveness is high! In the Lord's Prayer, it's no mistake that Jesus told us to ask to be forgiven our debts (or sins, or trespasses) as we forgive our debtors (or those who sin or trespass against us). We should expect to be forgiven in the way that we forgive. The Bible tells us that "if we confess our sins, He is faithful and just to forgive us..." (1 John 1:9a NIV). Should we be any less faithful and just when it comes to our neighbor?

Some people spend their whole lives carrying grudges. Those grudges effect their whole outlook on life. How much better would our lives be if we could just learn to forgive. Like a loving parent, God tells us everything He tells us to do for our own good. Carrying a grudge keeps us from experiencing all the joy He has to offer. Putting our grudges in the past allows us to be free to really experience that joy. Grudges are like piles of filthy rags that are piled over us, keeping our light from shining. Radically Real Christian, you are the light of the world. It is time to throw off that pile of filth and shine with the light of the Lord!

Forgiveness is a virtue that will pay dividends in your life. The things the world is seeking are all there in Christ. Peace, love and joy are the light that will draw people to you and to Christ. Forgiveness is the key. Remember the debt Jesus paid for you and joyfully forgive your neighbor and you will see your peace and your love and your joy multiplied as the light in you really begins to shine.

The Golden Rule

A big part of "walking the talk" is how we treat others. What we are really talking about here is living a life following after our example, Jesus. Jesus knew exactly how people were going to treat Him here and how His life would end. Yet His vision for people and their salvation led Him to carry on. He did not consider a person's importance in society. He showed kindness and compassion to all. Even on the cross with nails through his hands and feet, He asked the Father to forgive them. There is something to be learned here for Radically Real Christians on how to treat others.

The basic standard of decency is the Golden Rule, "Do unto others as you would have them do unto you." This is actually a paraphrase of Matthew 7:12. It is a command from Jesus and it deserves our utmost attention. The importance of this rule becomes increasingly apparent to the Radically Real Christian. The first thing to notice is the most important word in the phrase, "you would have them." Without those words, it is really just "Do unto others as (they) do unto you." That, unfortunately, is how many people choose to live their lives. It creates escalating tensions, vengeance (which the Lord reserves for Himself) and turmoil throughout the world. Ask yourself a question. What kind of world would it be if everyone just treated each other as they would like to be treated? I believe that it would be very close to Heaven on earth, if everyone were operating on true Christian ethics and morals. If we considered the people our actions would affect before we acted, how much better could we make our world? You see all actions have consequences, and not considering them before we act has always been a recipe for disaster. By considering the Golden Rule and carrying it out to the letter, we can save ourselves a whole lot of stress and aggravation.

There is a problem with the golden rule however and it is important that we have a look at it. It is not a problem with the rule itself. The rule is part of the Word of God and is not corruptible. The problem comes in with the fact that sinful people may misinterpret the rule. You see the Golden Rule is dependent on the moral framework of the person carrying it out. As the effects of sin run rampant, everything changes (except of course for God and His Word). An example of the Golden Rule being misused would be a corrupt government official. As a corrupt government official, they could feel quite comfortable offering a bribe, because they would be more than willing to accept one. They could do this and not violate the letter of the Golden Rule. They would merely be doing unto others as they would have others do unto them.

The Word of God and His ways must always take precedence. Obviously, a sinless God would never accept a bribe (though often times that is how we pray) for example. We can see from this example that judgement used in applying the Golden Rule must be tempered with our understanding of the heart of God.

The Radically Real Christian must always live by the Golden Rule, if he or she is to be effective at sharing the Gospel. Our moral foundation in God's word and the guidance of the Holy Spirit should always keep us centered and shelter us from making the wrong decision (as long as we obey their guidance, which is something Radically Real Christians should always seek to do). Just remember that the person we treat according to the Golden Rule may not necessarily reciprocate. That in no way should keep us from continuing on in the Golden Rule. We are called to be holy and righteous and to be a light in this world. People did not treat Jesus as He treated them, He loved them and they nailed Him to a cross for His trouble. He is the example we must live by if we want to be effective in doing His will. It is our mission as Radically Real Christians to model the attributes of Christ.

As we look back over this chapter a few things should "pop out." The first and most important thing is this: When you call yourself a Christian whether you want to or not, you represent Christ. Walking the talk 24 hours a day, seven days a week is your duty and obligation. The world is watching to see if you can do it. Remember, even though it may appear that they want to see you fail what they really want (by and large) is to see you succeed. They want the hope, joy and peace that Radically Real Christians have. If they see you living it, it will be a lot easier to show them the way. A Radically Real Christian must be quick to apologize when they fail. We must never walk away and hope nobody saw us.

People outside the church often look at us as hypocrites. They see our imperfections and say we don't mean what we say. It is important that when you are confronted with that argument, and if you witness, you will be confronted with it, that you have an answer. One of the best answers I have heard comes from a man from my church who has since gone on to be with the Lord. He always used to say that the church is not a country club for saints it is a hospital for sinners. None of us are perfect, and we should not pretend to be. We should strive to be perfect and we are made perfect in Christ but we should never put on airs about our own perfection. 1 John 1:8 reminds us that "if we claim to be without sin, we deceive ourselves and the truth is not in us." Instead of trying to convince others we are perfect and fooling no one, wouldn't it be better to strive for righteousness (in the Lord) and let others notice something special.

If you learn nothing else from this book, learn this, the world does not like perfect people. Look what they did to Jesus! What they really cannot stand is people who are pretending to be perfect. They will respond to someone who has been through the struggle they are going through and came out the other side. When they see this in you, they will want to know how you did it. You then have the golden opportunity to tell them about the One that led you through. If you witness in this way, you will not appear to be someone who feels superior, but rather a survivor with some real answers. Now let me make one thing clear. If you haven't been through what they are going through, don't make something up. That is still called a lie. It is the enemy's tactic and it will only lead to problems, even if your intentions are good. If you have not been there, just listen and show that you genuinely care. That is what Jesus did. He never sinned, and so He could not attest to how sin had messed up His life, but He could listen and He did help. That is how a Radically Real Christian lives and acts.

The Golden Rule also has another application. It means to put the needs of others before our own needs. It means that we show an uncommon politeness toward others. It means that when we get to the door, we hold it open for the person behind us. It means we let a person or two off of the exit ramp before we go. It means we stop to help the elderly person along the road with the flat tire. It means we go out of our way to make sure that the kid or the shut-in who doesn't have transportation makes it to the church. It means we go see that person who just lost a loved one and just listen. It means that we go the extra mile in whatever we do. Why? Because deep in our hearts we would want the same done for us. God also wants us to do these things for each other. In James, we hear that faith without works is dead. The Radically Real Christian's faith must be alive and well to really point people toward Jesus. Please keep in mind one other thing as, we serve, we must serve in the name of Jesus. We don't want people to think we serve just because we are good. We are not here to bring glory to ourselves. We are here to bring glory to God.

When you help someone, make sure that they know that Jesus has helped you. In some of the cases, of course you won't get time to share your faith. When you let a person off the exit ramp you can't (really) pull them over and say "I left you off because Jesus would have done it for me." You also shouldn't follow them home. Chances are that would really "freak them out." They would probably be too busy dialing 911 to hear your testimony. But there are things you can do. Put a bumper sticker or decorative plate on your car. At the door, when you let someone pass in front of you, may not be an opportune time to stop them and witness, (although if God gives you an opening please do) but you could wear your faith on your sleeve (so to speak). Buy a couple nice Christian T-shirts and wear them when you go out. Or perhaps you could get a piece of jewelry or something else that allows you, literally to wear his name. Some people may argue with this, but I believe that when you help someone and they see the name of Jesus on you, it plants a seed. There is another side to this too. When you are literally wearing the name of Jesus, you need to be even more careful how you treat others. You have an even better opportunity to live your witness when even strangers can see who you belong to.

A little while back, I mentioned helping others in need because when we are in need we would want help. This will actually ruffle some people's feathers. In western civilization, we are deeply based in being self-sufficient. We can do it all on our own and we need no one's help. Let me tell you something. Self-sufficiency is a joke. We cannot even breathe without God providing the air. We are totally dependent on God. Our motto has become "God helps those that helps themselves." Let me assure you that those words never EVER appear in the Bible. When we need help and it is offered, we should graciously accept it. The truth of the matter is that offering help is another person's way of ministering to us. Do not let your pride get in the way of someone else's ministry. Pride is of the devil and it has no place in the life of a Radically Real Christian (except for being proud of Jesus).

Maybe the person that ministers to you is not a Christian. Tell them as you thank them that you had prayed for someone to come and help. Tell them that you think God sent them to help you. Tell them about all the times in your life when God has helped you. Tell them about your hope and joy even in this difficult situation. Even in your time of need, you can be a powerful witness for the Lord. Never forget that. Maybe, in Christ, you can repay the person that helps you out with the gift that lasts forever, the gift of eternal life.

Never think for a minute that being a Christian makes you better than anyone else. God loves every person on this earth. Being a Christian does not make us better than non-Christians, it only makes us better off. We have a duty to share the gift we have been given with all that we come in contact with. Not all will choose to love Him but He loves them just as much as He loves you. We must see others that way.

It would eliminate so much sin in the world, if we could just see everyone we come into contact with as a child of God. Could we bypass the hurting without stopping to help? Could we look down on anyone, knowing that if it were not for the grace of God we could be in the "same boat?" Could we abuse others? Would racism exist? Could we lust after another person or look at pornography if we realized that the object of our lust was a child loved by God? Could we spread hurtful rumors or anything else? You fill in the blank. This is a key to success in a Radically Real life.

If you expect to fulfill your mission and reach people for the Kingdom, you must treat people as children of God. No matter who they are or what they've done or what they have, they are all sons and daughters of Adam, members of our family. We must lead people lovingly, just as Jesus does. Remember Jesus spent a lot of time with the very people that society chose to turn their backs on. Should we do any less? We need to look at His example as we interact with the rest of the world. Look at your attitude. Will a hurting person see love in your eyes or contempt? Radically Real Christians need to be role models to a hurting world so that we can lead them to the ultimate role model, Jesus Christ.

Radically Real Christians must also adopt a forgiving attitude toward everyone. It's not always easy but it wasn't easy to have nails driven through his hands and feet either and Jesus did that for you. Throw off the weight of your grudges and shine bright. Remember we have been forgiven much and our neighbors deserve nothing less. By showing forgiveness, we model something that has been missing for a very long time on this planet. It is one of the easiest ways to stand out in the crowd but it is not easy. Forgiveness is a lost art. Find it! In a world filled with people bent on getting even, you will be a breath of fresh air. Remember the forgiveness of God was not something we deserve and yet Jesus paid a high price to give it to us. Our neighbors are no less deserving, no matter who they are or what they have done. That was the attitude Jesus had and it must be ours as well.

Radically Real Christians can stay on the straight and narrow only in the power of God. We need to spend time with Him to successfully complete the mission He has set before us. We must constantly live as if someone is watching because someone always is.

Radically Real People from the Bible

The Good Samaritan

OK, I know what you're thinking. "The Good Samaritan was not a real person." You're right. Yet he was a character in one of Jesus' most powerful parables. Jesus used the Good Samaritan to challenge people to follow his example. This is a challenge to the church and especially Radically Real Christians to live to a higher standard. Let's have a look at the story.

A Jewish man is robbed, beaten and left for dead along the side of the road. Two respected members of the community see him lying by the road as they walk by. They see him lying there in a pool of his own blood, dying. Neither of these folks are willing to stop and help. Let's stop there for a moment.

In this parable, Jesus has something to say to the church. These two respectable people were clearly not living as they should have been living. Oh, I'm sure they were busy, important people, but they had a responsibility to help someone in need and they didn't. They neglected their duty. Christians are called to follow Jesus' example. We are called to go out of our way to help someone in need. How far out of our way? Well Jesus left heaven to come to earth to save you. He spent 33 years here trying to show us the way. I guess that means we should be willing to go pretty far out of our way. We should also remember how Jesus was treated for doing all of that and expect to sometimes be treated accordingly when we go out of our way to help. Jesus left the most wonderful place there is. He could have stayed in Heaven and let the world go to Hell (literally) but He didn't. He left the comfort of heaven and came to earth to be mistreated and misunderstood constantly. Eventually, he was spat upon, beaten and murdered by the very people He came to save. If Jesus could do all that, surely, we can leave our comfort zone and help our neighbor.

As we go back to our story, the man is still beaten and bloody, lying along the side of the road. The most respectable people of his community have just passed him by and left him to die. Then along comes the Samaritan. No self-respecting Jew at that time would allow himself to be touched by a Samaritan. They were considered to be vile, unclean heathens. They were in effect victims of racism to the extreme.

The Samaritan sees the suffering man and stops to help. Not only does he help the man and bind his wounds, but he also takes him to a "hotel" and pays the attendant to care for the man. Further he guarantees to come back and pay any other expenses on his next time through. Clearly the Good Samaritan was the one who was respectable here and his example is one that we must follow to be Radically Real.

Now the reason Jesus made his character a Samaritan was to shame his Jewish audience and make them realize that they were to be good neighbors and help those that are in need. If they didn't, then a lowly Samaritan would do what they should have done. (Note: Jesus did not feel that the Samaritans were "lowly," but He knew that His audience's prejudices would make them get the point of the parable.)

I maintain that there is another point to be gained from this story. The Good Samaritan would have been the victim of prejudice. He would have had every reason to hate the man in the ditch and just pass right on by. He could have repaid prejudice for prejudice. Yet that is not what He did at all. Even after generations of hatred and racism, he showed forgiveness to the man. He forgave all the abuse the Samaritans took from the Jews and showed mercy to a fellow human being that needed his help.

Radically Real Christians can learn a great deal from the Good Samaritan. We must forgive and show mercy because we have been forgiven and shown mercy. We must have no room for prejudice in our lives. We must go out of our way to help those in need because that is exactly what has been done for us. Do all of these things and you will be well on your way to being Radically Real.

Chapter 8

Live It, Learn It, Love It!

The Word of God--The Radically Real Road Map

All Scripture is God-breathed and is useful for teaching, rebuking, correcting and training for righteousness, so that men may be thoroughly equipped for every good work.

--2 Timothy 3:16, 17

I have to admit one of the really frustrating things today is how hard it is to get Christians into the Word of God. We give up so easily sometimes. We get to a point where God is going into great detail about the law or something and we give up. We don't see the application and so we lay it aside. This is a tragedy. God gave us His Word to strengthen us, to lift us up, to show us the way to live and more importantly the way to Heaven through His Son and yet so often we neglect it. Brothers and sisters, we have so much to learn from the Word of God. It is vital that we give the Word attention, every day. As you read these words, if you have not yet read the scriptures, get your bookmark out and place it here. These are the words of a mere man who struggles just like you. You need to spend time in the Word of God first. Having taken my own advice, I would especially recommend reading 2 Timothy 2:22-3:17

The book of Second Timothy is a book written by Paul to Timothy, a young pastor of the church of Ephesus. Paul is giving Timothy encouragement and advice. He tells Timothy to flee evil desires of his youth. Clearly, this is very sound advice as we so often have difficulty with temptation. Temptation is and always will be a trap, and there is certainly no weakness in fleeing from it. Paul tells Timothy to pursue righteousness, faith, love and peace. He tells us to avoid stupid arguments. Ouch, talk about stepping on toes. During the writing of this book, we received a resolution from one of the strangest elections in American history, the Bush/Gore presidential race. As I look back over this period, I think of how many times I allowed myself to get into political arguments instead of remembering that God was in control and seeking His will. Clearly, once my vote was cast, I had done all I could do. Any argument I got into after that point was clearly pointless and not worthy of the time I spent on it. He goes on to say that they produce quarrels and the Lord's servant should not quarrel but instead be kind to everyone. Once again, I must say ouch. This book (Radically Real), I am convinced, is written as much for me as for the reader.

As we continue to read the Scripture, we find Paul telling Timothy to gently instruct those who oppose him. Paul says Timothy should do this "in the hope that God will grant them repentance leading them to the knowledge of the truth and that they will come to their senses and escape from the trap of the devil who has taken them captive to do his will." (2 Timothy 2:25, 26 NIV)

I have to let you in on something here. The vast majority of this book was written between 4 and 7 a.m. This is the time of the day when I have real quiet time. My first step is always a lengthy period of prayer, and then I begin to write. As I began to write this morning, I was continually feeling led to the scriptures. Now the scriptures have been used heavily in the writing of this book, but this morning the leading was overpowering. I was unsure what to read specifically. So, I decided to re-read the passage I am basing this chapter on 2 Timothy 3. As I read, I became unclear on the context in which the text was written so I went back a few verses and found this passage. When I did that, I found out why the leading was so strong. You see verses 25 and 26 speak to something I really struggled with yesterday. (Radically Real Christians must always follow the leading of the Spirit especially when it pertains to the word of God.)

As I have previously mentioned, I am involved in youth ministry. One of the things I have done in this ministry was to create a web site for my group. I recently added a neat feature called a bulletin board. On it the members of the group and I can leave each other messages. I only had it online about two or three days (none of the kids had even placed a message on it yet), when I received a message from someone outside who wanted to deny the deity of Christ. It included a link to a site that had detailed "proof" of their argument.

Even though I believe none of it, my first thought was, "Oh great, just what I needed, something to confuse the kids." This reading has convicted me that I must research and do the work to defend my faith with the real facts, not just for my kids but so that maybe the sender (who is completely unknown to me) might read it and see the truth. Maybe this opponent will even come to Christ. Never discount the power of the Word of God and the leading of the Holy Spirit.

The encouragement to Timothy in the following verses is as important to us today as it was to Timothy. As we read it, I believe we find a lot of similarities to the world today. This is the timeless nature of the Word of God. Look at what Paul writes. "People will be lovers of themselves, lovers of money, boastful, proud, abusive, disobedient to their parents, ungrateful, unholy, without love, unforgiving, slanderous, without self-control, brutal, not lovers of the good, treacherous, rash, conceited, lovers of pleasure rather than lovers of God." (2 Timothy 3:2-4) Does this sound familiar? Is this first century Ephesus or 21st century America?

Paul goes on to describe people having a form of godliness but denying its power. This is the state much of the church is in. Many of us are not Radically Real. In regard to the Christian life many of us are saying one thing and living another. A major criticism of the church from non-believers for centuries has been that people in the church are hypocrites. While in some cases, we take exception (after all, "All have sinned and fallen short of the glory of God," imperfection is not hypocrisy) in many cases it is true. Christianity can never be lived as "do as I say, not as I do." We must live a life that reflects the values taught in the Word of God. Of course, the first step in that is reading and studying the Word of God. A Radically Real Christian's Bible may look a bit tattered, but it should never be dusty.

Paul then goes on to charge Timothy to stay strong in the face of persecution and encourages Him in the fact that God is always with us. He then goes on to give Timothy instruction on the importance of the Word of

God. He first tells us that all scripture is "God Breathed." This means, precisely, that although the Scriptures were written by the hands of men, they are spoken from the mouth of God, speaking to the writer through the Holy Spirit. It is for this reason that although the Bible was written by many writers, over the course of over thousands of years, the message runs neatly together. Skeptics may point to alleged discrepancies in the text, but if the reader is willing to do the required study, they will soon see that the Word is sound and consistent. For the most part, the Bible is very clear and concise in its meaning and we must be cautious that when we interpret it that we interpret properly. Always remember that in the Garden of Eden the fall of man was caused by Satan making Eve question whether or not God meant what He said. We must take God at His Word. He will not let us down.

The Word of God

For the most part, my attitude toward the scriptures is, "God said it, I believe it, and that settles it." Do I understand everything in the Word of God? Not by a long shot, but maybe I'm not meant to (at least not all at once). If I understood everything in the Word, I would no longer have to study it. And studying the Word of God brings us closer to Him. God says in His Word, for example, that He created the Universe in six days. I cannot understand how He did that. It is too big for my comprehension, but from the things I have seen Him do in my own life, I believe it. He proves himself to us in our lives if we believe and trust Him. Now, some will say to me that scientific evidence demonstrates that a six-day creation is impossible.

First of all, that is untrue. There is plenty of evidence, if we will open our eyes to it. (For answers on Creation, I will defer you to the experts, Answer in Genesis, www.answersingenesis.org.) Second, has science ever given me comfort when I was hurting? Did science ever sacrifice itself for me? Did science create me? Has science ever even dried one of my tears? No, God did all that. I will trust Him. Oh, and one more thing, the God breathed scriptures tell us in Matthew 19:26 that with God all things are possible. He didn't say "some" He said "all".

People find many things in the Word of God to be unbelievable. Scriptural stories like Jonah being swallowed by a giant fish, living in there for three days and then being spat out on dry land, or the story of the sea being parted before Moses and the children of Israel. In the natural world, these things just do not happen. Stories of Jesus' birth to the virgin Mary and him walking on water, turning water into wine and raising the dead seem implausible in the natural world. In fact, with all of our wisdom most of these things are impossible in the natural world. But remember this, we do not serve a natural, limited God. We serve a supernatural God through whom all things are possible.

It is vitally important that Radically Real Christians resist the temptation of putting God into a box. God is, to steal a term from business, outside the box. As a matter of fact, God made the box. He lives beyond our limitations and is capable of everything and anything. It seems to me that as we pray and study the Word of God and seek to serve Him that we would do well to remember that His unlimited power is at our disposal if we are truly doing His will. How many times do we tie the hands of God in our lives with our own disbelief? Remember, in His Word, Jesus reminds us that with God all things are possible. He also tells us about having faith the size of a mustard seed that we can tell a mountain to throw itself into the sea and it will. That should be enough for us to realize that we dare not put any limitations on God's power.

A lack of understanding on our part can never be misconstrued as a lack of power on God's part. Our lack of understanding should not ever discourage us but rather it should drive us even further into the Word of God. The greatest part of all of this is we will not be ignorant forever; the Word tells us that in Heaven all things will be made clear to us. Between here and there the Word of God is our friend and our guide and it is time we spent more time in it. It is more than just the bestselling book of all time, it is a way that God can communicate His unchanging Will to us.

Let's look a little closer at the passage from second Timothy. It says that the Word of God is useful for teaching. We can learn by the examples of the people in the Bible. The tendency among Christians sometimes is to look at these people as superhuman. They seem almost like superheroes. It is not necessarily wrong to view these people with respect, but to put them on too high a pedestal misses the point. These were real people, ordinary people who put their lives into the hands of a mighty, powerful, unstoppable God. The results are almost unbelievable, but they are entirely possible to a God without limits. To believe in God is to believe His Word. Anything less is unacceptable for the Radically Real believer. Let's look at a few of these people and see what we can learn from them.

Consider Noah. The world had become so corrupt that he and his family were literally the only people left alive that were serving God. Can you imagine what that would have been like? Sometimes, in the world you feel alone, knowing that there are millions of Christians in the world facing the all the same and even greater problems. Noah and his family alone stood with God. Imagine what it would be like if there were no church. Imagine that there is no one to fellowship with. No believers to come along side you when things get tough. That is what Noah was faced with. God told Noah to build an ark and, without question, Noah built an ark.

It was a remarkable achievement. It was 450 feet long, 75 feet wide and 40 feet high, about the size of a small cruise ship, built by one family out of wood with no power tools. It took 120 years to build. Can you imagine the ridicule Noah must have endured as he worked all those years to build this huge boat on dry land? Can you imagine the faith it must have taken for Noah to carry on? Imagine being one of Noah's sons in school while your dad is building a huge boat, miles away from any water.

It is important that we do not miss the symbolism in this story. The ark was a symbol of Salvation by faith for the whole world to see. You see Noah knew what God told him and he believed what God said. He had faith that what God said was true. But it was more than just faith, Noah put his faith into action. Noah didn't just believe, Noah started to build and when the ridicule of the people increased, Noah persevered and his faith increased. The world thought Noah was a crazy old man, a religious fanatic, but Noah knew the truth. God was giving the world that 120 years to clean up their act and get on the boat. Instead, the world ridiculed Noah and kept going down the path to destruction.

Things haven't changed much, the world still mocks God with impunity, but one day they will find themselves sealed "outside the boat as the raindrops start to fall." Can you imagine the panic on the day when people realize that God was not a joke? That day is coming again. There has been a symbol of salvation for the world to see for the last two thousand years in the cross of Jesus Christ, but the people ignore it or they mock it.

Radically Real Christian, the Ark has been built and it is time for us to be like Noah and fill the ark. Noah had his orders. He was to build the ark. His faithful obedience to God through ridicule and persecution is an example for us all. Likewise, we have our orders. We get them at the end of Matthew. Jesus told us to go into the world and make disciples of all nations. The Bible tells us that it is God's will that none should perish. That means if we have the faithfulness of Noah, we are to be out in the world reaching people for Christ. God used Noah's faithfulness to save the human race. Every person you have ever met in your life; every person that has lived since the flood has been a descendant of Noah. This is just one of the examples to live by that we can find in the Word of God.

Another example is Moses. Imagine this. You're the leader of a nation that has just been enslaved for over 400 years. You've just witnessed God break the back of the nation that has enslaved your people (incidentally the most powerful nation on Earth at the time) through a series of plagues. You have been a witness to the real supernatural power of God. The leader of the nation has just lost his first-born son in the last plague as well as every first born male and animal in his nation while your people remain unscathed. He is broken and he can take no more, so he decides that it is time to let your people go. You're leading the whole nation across the desert like some kind of gigantic parade. Little do you know back in the palace, the king has just had a rude awakening. He has just lost all of his slaves and he will not be able to complete all the grandiose projects he was going to build on the backs of your people. He starts to have second thoughts. Sure, he has lost everything, but he still has his pride and he wants his slaves back.

Just as you get to a large body of water, you hear a noise behind you that sounds like thunder and you turn to see the most powerful army in the world about to take your people back by force if necessary. You don't have time to go around the body of water and your people are not armed for a fight. In short, your goose is cooked. You turn to God and say, "Lord, I trust you immensely, I have seen your hand at work before, but.... HEEEELLLLLLPP!"

God tells you to raise your staff over the water. Not the most orthodox approach perhaps, but this is God after all. You do what God tells you and strange things start to happen. God, in a pillar of cloud that looks a bit like an F-5 tornado, runs interference behind you. A mighty wind begins to blow. Suddenly, the water begins to move until it forms two great walls with a dry path down the middle large enough to walk your people through on dry land.

Can you imagine how Moses felt when the waters parted? We can learn a lot through Moses, like us he was imperfect. He at one point committed murder when he saw one of his fellow Israelites being beaten. He probably had a price on his head in Egypt and yet Egypt was where God had called him to go. He had a speech impediment and in no way felt qualified to lead the people and yet God made him able. Moses had a lot of things going against him. He was 80 years old when God called him to lead the people out of Egypt and yet with all the things that he had going against him, He had God going for him. God did amazing things through Moses, because Moses was obedient and faithful. Remember what our passage says, "it (the Word of God) is useful for instruction." What we can learn from Moses is that if we are faithful and obedient to the call of God on our lives, He will likewise do amazing things through us.

The story of Moses and the Red Sea has come under attack in recent years. Scientists have been trying to explain this miracle of God away as a coincidence. Their basic premise is that during certain times of the year, in times of drought, the Red Sea becomes very shallow. Sometimes only inches deep. Their explanation is that a wind came up and blew the very shallow water and it was as if the people were crossing on dry land. The truth is that if you were to read the story only as far as I have gone here, the scientist's theory has some merit. The problem is I have left something out. If you go a little farther in the scriptures, you see that after the last of the Israelites got across the river, the Egyptian army followed the Israelites into the Red Sea, on the same dry land. When the whole army was in the Red Sea, it closed in on them and they all drowned. Now if you choose to believe the scientist (and you may if you want to, it's a free country), you must also believe that the most powerful army in the world, an army with horses and chariots and the most advanced weapons of the time, drowned is several inches of water. I think I will side with God on this one. Remember what Paul tells us 1 Corinthians 3:19,20: "For the wisdom of this world is foolishness in God's sight. As it is written: 'He catches the wise in their craftiness; and again, 'The Lord knows that thoughts of the wise are futile.'"(NIV)

And then there is Joshua, faithful, trustworthy Joshua. One of only two of the Israelites that crossed the Red Sea that were permitted to enter into the Promised Land. Everything was going fine until they came up to the great walled city of Jericho. It was here that Joshua received what may well be the strangest military orders ever given. Now I am sure from all I have read that

Joshua fully trusted God to give him victory over Jericho, but I would give anything to see the look on his face when God gave him the plan. Can you imagine what went through his mind when God told him just to march the people around the city every day for seven days? But you know what? Joshua trusted God. And when God told him how He wanted the job done, Joshua did it God's way. That is one of the biggest lessons we can learn from the Story of Joshua, God's way is the best way, the right way and the only way. He marched the people around the city, they blew their horns, the screamed when they were supposed to and that wall fell just like God said it would! Too often we live our lives like Frank Sinatra, you know..."I did it my waaaay!" The word of God in the example of Joshua tells us "my way" is overrated. It is time to do it God's way.

Imagine you are a frightened young woman. You've just been caught in adultery and now you are being dragged through the streets by a bloodthirsty mob. It's 30 AD so you're not going to end up as a cover story on the National Inquirer, you're about to be stoned to death. One of the mob throws you at the feet of a man. This must be the teacher Jesus that everyone is talking about. You don't realize it at the time, but the mob is really out to get Him and you are just a pawn in their little plot. You're just being used, as a matter of fact you may have even been set up to take this fall. The high and mighty Pharisees start listing off charges against you.

This Jesus is acting kind of strange. The Pharisees go on and on and on about the law and what the law demands but Jesus just sits there writing with his finger in the dirt. The Pharisees continue demanding until, finally, Jesus speaks. When He speaks, the words are the most amazing words you have ever heard in your life. He says, "Let him without sin cast the first stone." Strange things begin to happen. You have your head covered with your hands as you anticipate the pain of the rocks striking your flesh, but strangely, instead, you hear the gentle thud of rocks hitting the ground, one by one. It then becomes almost silent except for footsteps and a few words muttered under their breath as the mob disperses and walks away. You uncover your head to see Jesus with his hand outstretched to help you to your feet.

Something is missing. There is no trace of contempt in His eyes. There is only love and compassion. The two of you are standing alone in the middle of the street. He looks you in the eye and says, "Woman, where are they? Has no one condemned you?" You take one last look around. They really are all gone. "No one, sir," you reply. He says with Godly love in His eyes, "Neither do I condemn you, go and sin no more."

We can learn so much from Jesus in this story. Jesus knows the heart of all the people in that street. He knows their motivations. He knows your heart and mine in the exact same way. We too often are content to start picking up rocks when we see someone else in sin. We are very quick to forget our own sin, but here Jesus reminds us that there is only one who is sinless. Which brings us to another point. When Jesus said, "Let him without sin cast the first stone," He could just as easily have picked up a stone and thrown it at her. He was without sin and He would have been fully within His rights under the law to do just that. Jesus put His amazing grace and His sense of justice above his rights. Should we as sinners saved by His grace, be any less willing to put the common good before our own self-interest? Should we show any less grace than the perfect Son of God.

He also does not let the woman go without responsibility. This was not a "get out of jail free" card. He makes it very clear that she is to clean up her act from this time forward. As we get the forgiveness of God, it is imperative that we do everything in our power to "Go and sin no more" as well. These are just four of the hundreds of stories from God's Word that teach us how to live our lives and serve Him and our fellow man. The truth is that even these stories have far more to learn than the few things that I have touched on. One thing by now should be crystal clear. You cannot be a Radically Real Christian without spending some serious time in the Word of God.

God's Word, Paul says, "is also useful for rebuking correcting and training in righteousness so that the man (or woman)of God may be thoroughly equipped for every good work." If we say we are Christians, we had better be living the Word. As the saying goes, if you're going to talk the talk you better walk the walk. In this way, the Word of God keeps us accountable. If we see our brother in Christ going astray, we can use the Word to lead them back to the straight and narrow.

Sometimes the Word convicts us. It is easy to look at the things that go on in the lives of government officials and put them down. The Word tells us to pray for our leaders. We look at the extra- marital affairs that come up from time to time and we get all judgmental. Jesus tells us that if we look at a person of the opposite sex in the wrong way that it is as bad as having committed adultery with that person in your heart. Is there anyone on earth that can say they have never committed that sin. The word of God convicts us of our sin and helps us to do better.

Giving, Living, Loving

The Word of God is also an incredibly giving book. For one thing it gives hope. I think about all the hard times in my life when I have looked to Romans 8:28 for hope and comfort. "In all things God works for good for all those who love Him and are called according to His purpose." That is so incredibly hopeful. Think about it. Sooner or later, this thing that I am struggling with is going to work for the good of the Kingdom of God. My alcohol problem and the pain that came with it, which I brought on myself, is now useful as I minister to kids who struggle with the temptation to drink. God did not want me to drink and surely it was a sin and not in His will, but when I gave my life to Him, He took my past, spun it around and used it for good.

When I think of this verse, I also think about the Cassie Bernall story. The senseless carnage that occurred on April 20, 1999 is thoroughly unexplainable. And yet as we look at the situation, we see a young girl that a few days before her tragic death made a video telling about her commitment to Christ. After her death, people began to tell her story. That very video and her story were used to lead thousands to Christ. This makes the shooting no less senseless, but it does show that God is true to His Word and that even the most tragic situation can be used for good. Some will read this and say, "well why didn't God protect her?" The truth is I don't know for sure and I will probably never know why bad things happen to good people. When sin came into the world, all people paid the price. One thing's certain, however. When a Christian leaves this world, they are present with the Lord in a place where there is no more pain. That may well be the greatest hope of the Word of God.

God also gives us peace through His Word. The peace of standing over the body of a beloved family member who knows the Lord and knowing beyond the shadow of a doubt that you will see them again, happy and healthy and full of life. The grave is not the end for the Christian. When you can hold onto that, you will have a peace that passes all understanding.

God's Word gives us strength in times when we are weak. Weakness is subjective. We may seem stronger than someone else but we are all weak in the eyes of God because He is so powerful. His strength in us allows us to do much more than we are capable of on our own. One of my favorite examples of this is a quote I once heard from Governor Jesse Ventura. He made the comment that organized religion was for weak-minded people. This did not make me happy. My first thought was, "well if you elect a professional wrestler to be your governor, you get what you pay for." This was wrong on two counts: As mentioned earlier, we are to pray for our leaders and I should have especially have been praying that Governor Ventura would see his need for Jesus before it is too late and I failed to remember 2 Corinthians 12: 9,10, which states: "My grace is sufficient for you, for my power is made perfect in weakness, therefore I will boast all the more gladly about my weaknesses so that Christ's power may rest on me. That is why for Christ's sake, I delight in my weaknesses, in insults, in persecutions, in difficulties. For when I am weak then I am strong."

I am weak. I am even weak minded. I have tried to control my whole life on my own and I made a huge mess of it because I was outside of God's will for my life. When I gave control of my life to Jesus, that is when I really began to live. His power in my life is what makes everything so exciting. I am writing a book. That is not something I could do on my own. Who cares what Dave Weiss thinks about anything, but when I give it to God and say, "speak through me", that might be something worth reading. I preach; I used to have to have a few drinks so I could work up the nerve to announce songs from behind a DJ booth. Even after I gave up the drinking, I used to hide so I wouldn't have to read aloud in Sunday School because I got so nervous. God is the one that has made all the difference. Anything I have ever done well in my life has been a direct result of God working in my life.

In the youth ministry, I get to see a lot of God working in my weakness. I have been asked tough questions by my kids over many subjects that I had not prepared for, and somehow the answer comes seemingly out of thin air. Now psychologists and scientists may say that I had it stored in my memory and they might be right to a point, I read and study the Word a lot. But the bottom line really is this, someone helped me find it. It was God, He made me and gave me all I have. If believing in Him makes me weak-minded so be it, because I know He will reveal himself in my weakness. Radically Real Christian, we get stuck when we start to believe that we act in our own strength, we can't even make a hair grow on our own heads (as I approach 40 that is one skill I wish I had) God even provides the air we breathe. Rejoice in your weakness and let Him make you strong.

When it comes to living, God wrote the book! The Word of God is the guidebook to life. Think about it. From the fall of man in Genesis 3 forward to the end of time, God has it covered. Our questions are answered in this book. The Ten Commandments give us the backbone for a healthy and moral life. As you look at each one you will see its relevance in daily life. The first commandment tells us that we should have no other gods. This is explored more in depth in a later chapter, but how many lives have been destroyed by messed up priorities? The second commandment tells us not to make any graven images to worship. It makes sense doesn't it? I have no need to worship anything made by my own hands. I do sometimes wonder if all those pictures of dead presidents on little pieces of paper might be a graven image, at least in some people's lives. Thou shalt not kill and steal are self-explanatory. The validity "Honor your father and mother..." is evident in the breakdown of the family. Coveting is of course a big problem in our society, and it causes people to spend themselves into oblivion and bankruptcy, incomplete lives, divorce and a host of other things. In this one small passage alone, God communicates so many truths that we should be hard pressed to do anything without consulting the Word of God. Many of the other laws of the Bible are extremely useful in guiding our lives.

The Book of Proverbs contains so many truths. The big thing is they are simple truths, in a world that always seems to seek the most complicated of solutions. The Proverbs show us that most things are a lot simpler than they appear to be, but often we want to rationalize away our own sin and these simple truths get in the way. Whenever we read the Word of God, it is crucial that we come at it with the right attitude. If we come at it with a bunch of preconceived ideas, we can be tempted to read things into the scriptures that were not intended.

I belong to several list serve e-mail groups. One day a man sent a message that was filled with blasphemous statements all taken from out of context verses from the Word. The Words were not misquoted, they were just taken out of the context. Rest assured, God will not tolerate the misuse of His Word. He was not made by our hands; we were made by His. His Word is not to be tailored to our lives, our lives are to be tailored to His Word. The

Word of God will protect us from false teaching. It is vitally important that Radically Real Christians test everything they hear against the Word of God. Owning a Bible is nothing, unless the Bible is opened up and read.

One of the best passages in Proverbs tells us, I believe the best attitude a Radically Real Christian can have. It is Proverbs 3:5 and 6, " Trust in the Lord with all your heart and lean not on your own understanding. In all your ways acknowledge Him and He will make your paths straight." (NIV) In this verse God is telling us that there will be things in this world and even in His Word that we will not understand. When we come up to this point, it is vital that we study and try to understand, but also that we don't "just make something up." We cannot lean on our own understanding; our finite minds are far too simple to comprehend this universe. When we lean on God, we are leaning on the creator and sustainer of all things. He alone understands it all. In trusting Him, He will guide us and keep us on the right path.

The Word of God's best guidance in living comes from reading and following the example of Jesus. Jesus lived the only perfect life ever. He was the only person in the history of earth that never sinned. His life should be the guiding principle for the life of every Christian. "What would Jesus do?" may be used to the point of being a cliché, but it still should still be the first question asked before every decision a Radically Real Christian makes. Don't even give me the statement I hear sometimes that Jesus lived in another time, because Jesus lives today. His Spirit is guiding the life of every believer today. In reading the Bible, we get a very good sense of the character of Jesus. It is apparent in almost every situation what Jesus would do. The Bible may not say do not smoke crack, but it does tell you to not be drunk with wine, and it does tell you that the body is the temple of the Lord. Either of these, among others, should tell you what is the right thing to do.

The most important message for living comes in the salvation message. The Bible tells us that Jesus is the only way to heaven (John 14:6). It also tells us that it is God's will that none should perish and that Christians are to go into the world preaching the Gospel. These are our marching orders, He has made His Will known.

Lastly, the Bible is God's love letter to us. The law is made to show us our need for Jesus. In John 3:16, God tells us that He loves us enough to give His Son for us. He tells us that we are to cast our cares on Him because He cares for us. Think about that for a moment. The Creator of the universe cares specifically what happens to you. He is the loving Father that gave us a way out of our sinful lives. He gave us a way out of Hell at the price of His only Son. Folks, that is love!

He tells us, "Come to me you that are weary and heavy laden and I will give you rest". He wants a personal relationship with us. He wants to be actively involved in our lives. HE LOVES US!!

I remember one time when I was a traveling salesman. I hadn't been home in a week. I worked an ungodly number of hours. I was exhausted. I was depressed and I was done! I was just starting my three-hour drive home wondering how I was going to stay awake. I was also wondering what point there was in life, if I had to continue traveling away from home and working so hard. I turned up my radio to keep me awake and tuned in a Christian radio station. Almost as soon as I turned it on and heard the announcer say, "Come to me you that are weary and heavy laden and I will give you rest." An unexplainable peace came over me. I actually wept. I prayed the whole way home. It was as if God said, "look Dave, things are tough right now, but I care. I am getting you ready for something special. It's going to be great, because I love you, trust me, you're going home." God's Word tells us of His great and perfect love for us. We need to be in the Word every day if we are going to be successful at living the life and completing the mission that God has for us.

The enemy comes against us so often and tries to attack us by telling us how worthless we are. The Word of God tells us that the Creator and Sustainer of the universe cares so much about us specifically, that He gave

His only Son that we might be saved. That means we are valued children of the most important being in the universe. Let me ask you a question, Radically Real Christian, who are you going to believe? I choose to believe the Word of God.

Reading the Word, studying it and then living what it teaches is one of the marks of a Radically Real Christian. God's Word never comes back void, but we must read it. We must store it in our hearts so that it will be there when we need it.

Power of Prayer

Prayer is one of the most important spiritual disciplines of the Radically Real Christian. It is our direct connection to the Creator of all things. If we omit prayer in our lives, we do a serious disservice not just to God but to ourselves as well. We get so busy that prayer seems to slip right out the door. So many things seem more important, but I maintain that prayer is the most important thing you have to do, so do it first. The Bible tells us to pray without ceasing. That is better than any advice I can give.

For the purposes of this chapter, I wanted to mention prayer in the context of reading God's Word. You see I believe the most effective way to read the Bible is after fervent prayer that God will show you something important that you can apply to your life. That is the key. We need to be asking God what He wants us to learn. We must pray that He will open our eyes to the truth that lives on the pages. Also ask God to help you to focus and concentrate.

Then after we read, we must look at what stood out to us. If we find ourselves convicted of a sin in our lives, we must pray that God will forgive us and help us to resist the temptation in the future. Maybe after reading God's Word, you will feel inspired to do something. Ask God to give you the wisdom and the ability to do what He has put on your heart. Do not resist the call of God. If He puts something on your heart while reading the scriptures, do it.

That being said, it is easy to tell whether He put it on your heart or if it was just an idea that popped into your head on your own. The first thing you need to do is, if there is any question, check it against the Word of God. There is only one thing God cannot do and that is sin. If your idea will cause you to commit a sin, it is not of God, PERIOD! Then ask if it will advance the Kingdom. This is a question for God, not your own head. Things that sometimes seem as though they will have no impact, can have a tremendous impact when put into the hands of a mighty God.

Lastly, pray that God will give you the courage and the opportunity to share what you have learned from His Word with someone that needs to hear the truth. Radically Real Christian as you will remember from the chapter on the full armor of God, the Word of God is the only offensive weapon you have, the sword of the Lord. Keep it sharp. Read it every day, memorize it, study it and live it. The battle is on, but your weapon is mighty. Used properly it will help you to emerge victorious.

Radically Real Examples from the Bible

Psalm 119

Psalm 119 is the longest chapter in the Bible. It speaks about, guess what...? The Bible! While I highly recommend you open your Bible and read it for yourself, I am going to highlight a few of the key verses to show you a few points on the importance of the Word of God.

We'll start with the first three verses. "Blessed are they whose ways are blameless, who walk according to the Law of the Lord. Blessed are they who keep his statutes, and seek Him with all their heart. They do nothing wrong, they walk in his ways." (NIV) God promises His blessings to those who walk according to His law and keep His statutes and seek Him with all their heart. The way we know the laws and statutes so we can keep them is by reading and studying the Word of God. And how can you seek Him with all your heart if you do not seek His will by reading the instructions that He gave for you. The easiest way to seek Him is to look where He told you to look. Some would argue that these laws are not for today because we live under grace now. They would, of course, be right but while we may not necessarily be under the law, there are still many things in the law that are for our own good and application can be made to our lives today. The Word of God is still the Word of God.

Going down to verse 9, we see "How can a young man (or woman) keep his way pure? By living according to your Word." (NIV) All we need to do is look at our society or watch the TV news for a matter of minutes and you will see the results of impure living. Keeping our way pure is crucial if we want to live a life that is pleasing to God and attractive to people seeking the truth. God tells us how to live a pure life in His Word. (Are you starting to see a pattern here?)

Verse 11 will be one of your memory verses. If you have not memorized this verse yet, stop reading and start memorizing! "I have hidden your Word in my heart so that I may not sin against you." Here is a key verse. You can't carry your Bible with you in everything that you do. You need to have the Word in your heart. You need to know that all things work for good of those who love Him who are called according to His purpose when things are going wrong. You need to remember to love your neighbor as yourself when your neighbor cuts you off on the highway. You need to remember to turn the other cheek. You need to remember that vengeance belongs to the Lord. And what if that person that you have been praying for forever finally comes to you to ask you about Jesus and you are miles away from the Word of God? The Word of God will keep us from sinning and it is crucial that we have it stored in our hearts but it is just as crucial to remember those life instructions that it brings.

We touched on this earlier, but in verse 28 "my soul is weary with sorrow, strengthen me according to your Word." (NIV) There is strength for the hurting in the Word of God. We can find amazing hope in the words of the Lord. One verse that comes to mind is that the sorrow may last for the night but the joy comes with the morning. God tells us in Psalm 30 that He can and will make it better if not in this life, then (for the believer) in the next. Psalm 119:50 also touches on this, "My comfort in my suffering is this, Your promise preserves my life." (NIV) (again, see Romans 8:28) God is faithful and keeps his promises. You may go into the Valley of the Shadow of Death, but the good shepherd will not let you stay there. He will take you through.

So often we hear about bad things happening to good people. This is one of the great mysteries that people face. A few answers were brought to light in Psalm 119. Verse 67 tells us, "Before I was afflicted, I went astray, but now I obey your Word." (NIV) Sometimes we bring our afflictions on ourselves. So many times I have heard people blame their circumstances on God and then proceed to list the many things they did to cause their own problem. We must realize that actions have consequences. Sometimes the consequences of those actions are enough to wake us up and put us back on the straight and narrow. This seems to be what happened to the writer of Psalm 119 because look at what he says in the following verse (68): "You are good and what you do is good. Teach me your decrees." (NIV)

The other thing that could be said is that God is good. He has no ability to do evil. Sometimes when we look at circumstances beyond our control, we forget how God sees the big picture. We must always remember that God is good and that in spite of whatever situation we find ourselves in, God cares for us. In verse 71 we see another turn on this. "It was good for me to be afflicted, so that I might learn your decrees." (NIV) So often we look at situations and fail to see what good can come of it. But like the child that burns their hand touching the stove and learns a valuable lesson, so do our own circumstances sometimes humble us so that God can work on us.

Perhaps the most famous part of this scripture can be found in verse 105. "Your Word is a lamp to my feet and a light for my path." (NIV) That is a profound statement. The Word of God is a lamp to your feet. It doesn't always illuminate the whole path so that you can see everything that is going to come along, but it does provide enough light for you to see where you are at the moment and where to place your next step. It lets you see the trail markers left by the people that have gone before. The Word of God will help you find your way from the wide road that leads to destruction and will help you to navigate the narrow road that leads to Heaven.

Radically Real Christian, life is like one of those wilderness orienteering races. There are many paths but only one leads to where you want to go. The Spirit is your compass and the Bible is your map. Without them you can easily lose your way. Do not neglect the Word of God. It is crucial to running the race successfully and getting the prize at the other end.

Chapter 9

Whose Are You?

Picking the Radically Real Path

But Seek First His Kingdom and all these things will be given to you as well.

--Matthew 6:33

Be self-controlled and alert. Your enemy the devil prowls around like a roaring lion seeking whom he might devour. Resist him, stand firm in the faith, because you know that your brothers throughout the world are undergoing the same kind of suffering.

--1 Peter 5: 8-9

What shall we say, then? Shall we go on sinning that grace may increase? By no means! We died to sin; how can we live in it any longer? Or don't you know that all of us who were baptized into Christ Jesus were baptized into his death? We were therefore buried with him through baptism into death in order that, just as Christ was raised from the dead through the glory of the Father we too may live a new life.

--Romans 6:1-4

He who is not with me is against me, and he who does not gather with me scatters.

--Luke 11:23

Choices, we make them every day, from hard choices like who to marry, to easy ones like what color socks to wear. Some choices are of almost no consequence whatsoever. Other choices are a matter of life and death. But there is one choice that is not only a matter of life and death it is much more than that. It is the choice of who we are going to follow, God or Satan. That choice is of eternal significance. Choose carefully.

This is not a new choice. As a matter of fact, we see the effects of poor choices all the way back to Genesis chapter three, when Eve made the choice to follow the serpent rather than to obey God. I wonder if she had any idea what the ramifications would be of that decision. I wonder if she realized that that one decision would affect her descendants for all time. The choices we make have consequences and some of them will go on forever.

Near the end of his life, Moses laid it out for the children of Israel in no uncertain terms. The choice that he set before them still lays before us today. Look what he said in Deuteronomy 30: 15 - 20:

See, I set before you today life and prosperity, death and destruction. For I command you today to love the Lord your God, to walk in His ways, and to keep his commands, decrees and laws; then you will live and increase. And the Lord your God will bless you in the land that you are entering to possess.

But if your heart turns away and you are not obedient, and if you are drawn away to bow down to other gods and worship them, I declare to you today that you will certainly be destroyed. You will not live long in the land you are crossing the Jordan to enter and possess.

This day I call heaven and earth as witnesses against you, that I have set before you life and death, blessings and curses. Now choose life, so that you and your children may live and that you may love the Lord your God, listen to His voice, and hold fast to Him. For the Lord is your life, and He will give you many years in the land he swore to give to your fathers, Abraham, Isaac and Jacob.

--Deuteronomy 30: 15-20 (NIV)

The choice the children of Israel were forced to make is the same one you and I face today. The choice is simple, choose to follow our Lord and live forever or choose to follow the enemy and suffer the consequences of our choices to the grave and beyond. To follow the real God to an abundant life, a promised land, a land of milk and honey or to follow false gods to a meaningless life of materialism and fear and suffering, death and separation from God. The choice seems so simple and yet people by the thousands make the wrong choice every day. Why? I believe it is because the enemy makes the wrong choices look easy. We see people that seek to follow false gods, like money and power, make gains. We see them seem to prosper. We see them have stuff that we want, and we start to wander toward the wrong tree. We start to see the forbidden truth and it looks like it would be good to eat. Then "old scratch" comes along and makes us question whether or not God really meant what He said and before you know it, we are out of Eden. We are outside the path that God has made for us, and we are enslaved by sin.

Were it not for Jesus, we would all be slaves, now and forever to the wrong choices that we make. But you see Jesus came and gave us a way out. Jesus gave us a u-turn, a way out of the world, a way back to the promised land. A way back to eternal life. Once again, we have set before us a choice: a choice between life and death, a choice between blessings and curses. The choice is yours alone. Choose wisely, choose life, choose Jesus, choose eternal life.

It is my hope that if you are reading this, you have already made your choice to follow Jesus. If you haven't, I urge you to go back to the chapter on conversion and pray the prayer that is there. Ask Jesus into your heart, today! Choose life.

As I have mentioned previously, I am a youth leader. I spend a lot of time with kids. One day I remember one of my girls came up to me pretty distraught and said, "Someone at school today called me a Jesus Freak." I thought for a minute and then said (sympathetically), "good!" I got one of those looks that says, "What are you talking about, Dave?" Think about it. If someone calls you a Jesus Freak it means they know who you belong to. Radically Real Christian, any name someone calls you that lumps you with Jesus is a badge of honor. It means that they associate you with Jesus. That is an awesome thing but it is also an awesome responsibility.

It means that you have become, like it or not, a physical representation of Jesus. What they see you do reflects on Jesus. As the old saying goes, "you are the only Jesus some people will ever see." How are you representing Him today?

Let's face it. We all sin! Every Christian is a sinner saved by grace. And yet, the world out there has no concept of grace. The very standards that they do not want you to apply to them, they will readily apply to you. Once you take the name of Christ, you are judged by a different set of standards. It may sound unfair, but Jesus dealt with the same thing. He was out there healing and casting out demons and what did the Pharisees say? They said, "He casts out demons by the prince of demons." Even though He was doing great good the people stood against him. Think about what that really means. Their blindness to their own sin made them stand against God. Is our society going to be any different?

No Middle of the Road

If you look at the scriptures one thing becomes abundantly clear. There is no room on the fence for the Christian, especially the one that seeks to be Radically Real. We need to be on one side of the other. We are either on the narrow road that leads to eternal life or we are careening down the wide road that leads to destruction. The key to the right choice is what you are seeking. There are a lot of choices to be made, but we must choose carefully.

In Proverbs 14: 12, King Solomon gives the warning that should be heeded. He writes, "There is a way that seems right to a man, but in the end, it leads to death." (NIV) We see this around us every day. Satan makes the wrong choices seem very appealing. Revenge seems like the answer when we have been wronged. Oh, how badly we would like to make people pay, but in the end all it brings is escalation and pain. It seems right to be tolerant of all the choices people make. It seems right that we should seek to sin without consequence. It seems right to work your life away to acquire more and more stuff. It seems right to live for the "good life." And yet all these choices can lead to the wrong road, the road that leads to death.

Think about it. Tolerance is a god for much of our society. We are called by our society to tolerate any and all lifestyle choices no matter how absurd or destructive it may be. Better to let people, like lemmings, charge off of the cliff than to speak up and say, "Hey buddy, you're going the wrong way." For some reason, the only thing not to be tolerated is holding to a standard of right and wrong. Not dealing with the consequences of our choices, or maybe better stated, sin without consequences, has become the battle cry of so many people. Yet, like it or not, no matter how hard we try to put it off, our actions do have consequences. We try to turn people that make bad choices into victims of circumstance to absolve them of responsibility for their choices. Whether we want them to or not, the consequences come to call.

Those who work their lives away for the acquisition of more stuff are doing nothing more than serving a false god and trying to fill a void that cannot be filled. They end up on their death bed with regrets not over stuff they haven't acquired yet, but rather over the real moments in life they have missed. And Satan laughs. The "good life" ends unfulfilled. The wrong road comes to its dead end.

If you are reading this book and you are on the wrong track, I have good news. "You ain't dead yet!" You have time to turn around, cross the median strip and enter the narrow road. The light you see at the end of that road is not an oncoming 18-wheeler, it is home!

If You're Not for Me You're Against Me!

Jesus makes it plain and simple. He tells us that there are only two ways to go. You are either for Him or you're against Him. There is no room for "waffling" here. If you choose not to decide, you still have made a choice. Think about the Deuteronomy passage we looked at a little while back. The choice was between life and death. Think about it. There is no "sort of dead". You're either breathing or you're not. You either are a Christian or you're not. You're either heaven-bound or you're not. And if you're not sure if you're a Christian, you're not.

It's easy enough to tell for sure. Do you love Jesus? Do you believe He is the Son of God? Do you believe He died on the cross? Do you believe He rose again? Do you believe He did it for you? Do you accept His free gift of salvation, the one He paid for with His life? Have you asked Him to come into your heart? (He said, "Behold I stand at the door and knock.") If you can answer "yes" to all of those questions, you are a Christian. If not, you are not. Pray and ask Him to help you with your unbelief, then ask Him into your heart. Close this book and do it now. Do not wait. Be for Him. He is for you.

So, If There's Grace Why Can't I Just Do Whatever I Want?

It really is not a bad question. If God is going to show grace to us as Christians, why can't we do whatever we want? The answer is very simple, when we give our lives to Christ we belong to Him. That grace that was so freely given came at a high price. The devil likes to make us forget that. He'd rather see Christians out there in the world living hypocritically, so that no one would be attracted to Christ. It is one of Satan's oldest tricks. He keeps using it because it keeps working. If you don't believe me, ask yourself this question: "How many "unchurched" people do you know that stay away from the church because they have been hurt by someone who calls themselves a Christian?"

As Paul tells us in Romans 6:1-4, we cannot go on sinning because when we come to Christ we die to sin. This is not to say that we will never again commit a sin. We all stumble from time to time, but it is urgent that we stay with God, that we hide His word in our hearts so that we may not sin against Him.

Satan hates you. He hates you so much that he will do everything he can to mess you up. He especially hates it when Christians are on fire for the Lord and live to serve Him. He will put up stumbling blocks in front of you to make you fall. Not so he can take your soul. If you are saved by the blood of Jesus, he cannot touch your soul, but so he can destroy your witness. We must put pride behind us. We must ask forgiveness both of God and of our neighbor and we must do it quickly. We must always go above and beyond to make sure that once we call ourselves Christians, we are doing everything to the glory of God and not to bring slander on His Holy Name. We must also make sure that we spend time in the Word and especially in prayer, so that we are constantly connected with the source of all righteousness. That is the best way to show the world who you belong to. That is the best way to be Radically Real.

Good Shepherd... Roaring Lion, you Decide!

Jesus said, "I am the good shepherd that lays down His life for His sheep." If we don't know a lot about shepherding, (and who does?) we may miss the meaning of this. Shepherds did more than just sit and watch sheep all day. They were the protector of the flock. They had to fight off wild animals, like wolves, lions, etc., for the protection of the sheep. This was in the days before the high-powered rifle when they had to fight them off with slings and arrows. They put themselves in great personal danger to do this. Jesus literally did this for us. Look at the passage from 1 Peter again. What does Peter compare Satan to? "A roaring lion seeking whom he might devour."

Now think about our Good Shepherd again. There you are, a sheep among the flock. Out of the corner of your eye, you see something really appealing, over by the edge of the woods. Maybe, it's some clover flowers that just look so good. Maybe it's that hot, little ewe you've been eyeing up for quite some time, and there she is, over there all by herself. Whatever the temptation, you leave the flock to pursue it. As you get a little way outside the flock, you hear a rustling behind you. At first it is faint, you look around and see nothing, so you keep going. As you get further away the rustling begins again only this time it is much louder. As you turn to look, you hear a loud roar and turn to see the biggest, ugliest lion you have ever seen, bearing down on you. You try to run, but you are terrified and besides you're a sheep. You're not built for speed, you're built for, well, wool. There is only one thing you can do. BAAAAAAAAAAAAH!!! Just as the lion goes for your throat a shepherd's crook grasps him around the neck and the battle is on.

The shepherd fights mightily, but it appears that the battle has gone to the lion. The shepherd's lifeless body lies on the ground, and the lion returns his gaze to you. He licks his chops and slowly stalks. You bleat loudly, but who will hear your call? You are about to be lion stew. The lion pounces and knocks you rolling to the ground. You feel his paws on your shoulders as saliva drips from his putrid mouth. You see blood-stained fangs as he opens his mouth to clamp it around your throat. You feel his hot breath on your wooly neck. The end is here. But no. Instead, the lion falls with a thud, and you look up to see your shepherd standing over you, holding his weapon, a blood-stained piece of wood. You are saved.

That's what it is like. Jesus is the Good Shepherd. Satan is a roaring lion and we are all stupid sheep that wander away from the flock. All we have to do is cry out to Him and He will come running and He will fight to save us. It may even look like He is defeated, but make no mistake about it, on the day that He rose from the dead, He proved beyond the shadow of a doubt that victory was ultimately his.

It all comes down to choices. God, by His very nature is love. He loves us. He wants us to love Him. He could make us love Him, by force, but that would really not be love. So, He gives us the choice whether or not we will love Him and follow Him. God also has a competitor for our love that He allows to exist. An angel, who decided in His pride long ago that He would ascend and take God's throne away. An angel made blind to the love of God, by his own beauty and fell to earth. That angel was Lucifer. He became Satan. He'd like you to believe that he is the equal to God, but He isn't. He is a counterfeit. He has never had an original thought.

Satan is not the equal of God. God has no equal, but a weird thing happened. We are like sheep, really, really dumb. Satan figured out that we all have weaknesses, and that if he dangled those weaknesses in front of us we would follow him. It worked like a charm. He started to convince us that his way was better and less restricted. Sheep also don't see real well, and we don't see the pitfalls that lay between us and the stuff he offers. The sheep started turning into lemmings and falling off the cliff. But Satan is not God and unlike God, he can't see the whole picture either. God had a plan. He would send a Savior, a Shepherd that would call His lost sheep back to Him. A Shepherd that would give His life for His sheep. That Shepherd was Jesus.

Satan thought Jesus would be easy to defeat. He came as a baby. A poor defenseless baby. "No problem," Satan thought. He went to Herod and said, "Herod, there is a kid out there, a little baby, who is destined to take your throne away. He's just a baby, now. Kill him while you have the chance." Herod, unable to find Jesus, had every little boy two years old and younger killed. But God was watching and Jesus was in Egypt by then.

As Jesus grew, you can bet, Satan plotted and schemed, but Jesus won out. Then it came to the time before Jesus was ready to take on His earthly ministry. You can bet by now Satan was getting desperate. Then he had another idea. If you can't beat Him, corrupt Him. Jesus went into the desert to fast for forty days. Satan tried every trick in the book, but Jesus had a book of His own, the Holy Scriptures locked away in His heart. Once again, Satan was defeated.

Satan's next thought almost worked. "OK, Jesus is tough, but look at these guys that are following him, maybe I can get Him through one of them. Which one looks greedy?" He settled upon the group's treasurer. "He likes those shiny coins a little too much, PERFECT." Satan started to whisper things in his ear. "He keeps talking about dying, how will you benefit if He dies. What will all this following Him get you if He dies? There'll be no powerful position for you, no money, no women. They'll think you're a fool.

You followed Him. You thought He was the Messiah. You thought He would overthrow Rome. How can a dead man overthrow Rome. You fool, He's no Messiah." Satan got through to Judas' pride and won His heart and Judas betrayed Jesus. The roaring lion had another kill, this time one from among the twelve. Satan was giddy with delight. "I've got you now, Nazarene. Let's see you get out of this one."

Well, you know the story from there. Jesus was tried before the Pharisees. Satan got them long ago, replacing God with pride and legalism. Then Jesus went before Pilate and Satan hit a little snag. You see Pilate had only one allegiance, and that was to Pilate. He knew Jesus was not guilty and that the people were against Him for no good reason. So, Pilate thought to Himself, "How will this look if this innocent man, a prophet, is crucified? What if His followers rebel and cause an insurrection? How will that look to Rome?" So, Pilate came up with an idea. "It's the custom to release one of their prisoners at this time. I'll put this murderer Barabus up to be released in place of Jesus. They'll never pick Him to be released." Satan worked overtime in the crowd that day, and all that work culminated in one word, "CRUCIFY." Then Satan went to work on Pilate. Allegiance to self is really allegiance to Satan, so it wasn't that tough. All Satan had to say to Pilate was, "The people want Him dead. Wash your hands of Him. It's not your fault." Jesus was headed to the cross and Satan was picking out his new throne. Heaven was his. Victory was his!

That Friday, Satan strutted around the throne of Grace like an evil peacock. Arrogance dripped from his voice as He said, "Where's your Son, God?" An evil laugh was emitted from deep within the fallen angel. He laughed harder and harder as Jesus struggled for every breath. He howled when Jesus said, "It is finished." "It sure is," Satan replied, "It's over, God, He is finished, He's dead, YOU LOSE!!!" "Where's your Son, God?" God did not reply. Then Satan left to torment the disciples some more.

Saturday rolled around. Satan again returned to the throne room. "What's the matter with you, God." "Do their Sabbath prayers bring you no joy? Where is your son, God? Where is He teaching today? Oh, that's right, He's not teaching anywhere? He's DEAD!!!" Satan laughed a laugh that rumbled the heavens. "I'll let you have your Sabbath, but tomorrow, it's all mine!!" Again, God did not reply.

Sunday morning came. Satan walked arrogantly and spitefully before the throne. "Are you still here? Give it up. It is finished. I'm taking over just like I said I would. Where is He? Where is your champion? Where is the one that you sent to defeat me? Oh, I'll admit it, He was pretty good, but He was just a man. I figured you would have at least made it interesting and sent Michael. But Jesus, He was a good man, He might have even been perfect, but He was no match for me." Then Satan snarled and said, "Where's your Son, God?"

But this time, Satan noticed something different. The old twinkle was back in God's eye. God said, "Satan, before you make yourself too comfortable, I think you better go and check the tomb." Satan laughed, "You're stalling, but I'll humor you." Satan stepped through time to the tomb. Something was wrong. The stone was moved. He went in. There was no body. "This has got to be a trick," Satan thought as a chill ran up his spine. He raced back to the throne. Panic was in his voice as he said, "Where's your Son, God?" God looked at him and smiled. "Where's your son, God? Please tell me. Where is He?" All of the sudden a bright light shone behind Him. It was a light so bright, brighter than any angel. "Oh No!!! It can't be." "I'm right here Satan. You put me through a lot, but I have one question for you, Devil, is that all you've got?" "Be gone from this throne room. Your days are numbered, beast." Then Satan returned to earth, defeated and angry.

That of course was not a biblical account and yet, hopefully some of it rings true. Satan has a two-fold attack. His first attack is to try to keep the lost, lost. He attacks them. He tells them they are no good. He convinces them that they are worthless or he lets them get enough stuff that they don't feel a need for God. His ultimate plan is the destruction of as many as possible. You see Satan knows he is on the losing end of this battle. He knows his future is in the place that was prepared for him and his angels and he wants to take as many souls with him as he can. You don't have to fall to him. If you are not a Christian you can ask Jesus into your heart. Jesus has already won this battle; the prophets have foretold it.

The second prong of Satan's attack is for the saved. You see, once you are saved by the blood of Jesus, Satan cannot have you anymore. So the next attack is on your witness. He will attempt to get you to sin. He will throw temptations at you. He will try to depress and defeat you. He will mess up your life and make you feel powerless, if he can. He will make you the kind of Christian that reflects badly on the Father so that the lost will not be drawn into the fold through your witness. The good news is you don't have to fall into this trap either. The Bible tells us very clearly that greater is He that is in me than he that is in the world. Jesus is bigger. Jesus is tougher. Satan may be an angel, but Jesus is God.

So whose are you? The answer should be easy. One is the good shepherd. One is a roaring lion looking to make a meal of you. One is the personification of love and the other, evil. One is the Son of God. One is the father of lies. The choice is simple, Radically Real Christian, choose life!

Radically Real Examples from the Bible

Joshua

Joshua was a born leader. From the time Joshua was a young man, he followed God. When spies were to be sent to the Promised Land, it was Joshua (and Caleb) that trusted God to give the land he had promised. His trusting of the Lord was what made it that he was one of only two of the people that God led across the Red Sea to ever enter the Promised Land. All the rest lost heart to the point where they wanted to stone Joshua. This teaches our first lesson, taking a stand for God may not always be popular, but it is always right.

As we stated earlier, Joshua became the leader of the Israelites after Moses and led the people across the Jordan to take the Promised Land. Then Joshua got an order that had to test his trust in God. When the Israelites approached the great walled city of Jericho, it was an almost impenetrable fortress. Joshua knew that he would have to take the city but one could imagine that he did not expect to do it in the way that God asked him to. First of all, an angel of the Lord came to Joshua and told him that God had delivered Jericho into His hands. From that point on there was no doubt in Joshua's mind that God would do exactly what He said He would. Then Joshua got what may be the strangest military order in history. He was to march around the city every day for six days. On the seventh day, they were supposed to march around the city seven times, have seven priests blowing trumpets, at the end of the seventh "lap" the priests were supposed to blow one long trumpet blast and all the men were supposed to shout and the walls would fall down. It sounds like a strange order, but the order came from God and Joshua trusted. God once again proved Himself to be trustworthy. Joshua was faithful to God, and with God's help the Israelites took the Promised Land.

Years later, as Joshua became older, and neared the end of his life, the people had settled the land and they got comfortable. Whenever we get comfortable, it seems as though we forget about our dependence on God. The people were beginning to look to the idols of the people that God had helped them drive out. They were no longer all for God, so of course they were turning against Him and the roaring lion was beginning to prowl.

It is in this environment that Joshua calls the people together. And after reminding them of everything God has done for them, Joshua lays it all on the line for them and calls them to make a choice. They could choose to serve the lifeless, handmade gods of the Amorites, or they could serve the Lord that gave them the land. Then Joshua makes the declaration that sums up the way he lived his life, "As for me and my household we will serve the Lord."

The question for you Radically Real Christian, is can you make that same statement? Can you boldly say that even if I am the only one, I will serve the Lord?

Chapter 10

Where Your Treasure Is

Radically Real Priorities

Do not store up for yourselves treasures on earth, where moth and rust destroy, and where thieves break in and steal. But store up for yourself treasures in heaven, where moth and rust do not destroy, and where thieves do not break in and steal. For where your treasure is there your heart will be also.

--Matthew 6: 19-21

How many times have you seen it? People on TV willing to do all kinds of ridiculous stunts for a shot at money, a car, fame, etc. The show Fear Factor comes to mind. People putting aside their greatest fears in exchange for a wad of money. People lying in vats filled with snakes and spiders and rats, eating some of the most disgusting things imaginable and doing death defying stunts that are very dangerous even with the aid of safety equipment. Why do the contestants do it? Because in the long run, they find something more important than their greatest fear. They are willing to put it all on the line for money.

In the 1996 presidential elections, the members of one party wore buttons that said, "It's the economy, stupid!" Their reason for wearing these buttons was quite simple, the nation had fallen into a moral cesspool, but the economy seemed to be the best it had been in a while so all else was fine. After the election it seemed apparent that the majority of the people agreed that it didn't matter what happened as long as we had money. Morality and virtue had become secondary to the almighty dollar.

In 1972, the Roe vs. Wade decision made abortion a right. No longer did a woman have to let the consequences of her own actions interfere with her ability to acquire the American dream of convenience and prosperity. No longer did men have to take responsibility for their actions. They could simply spend a few dollars at the local clinic and get on with their lives. No longer was the question of "do I love this person enough to spend my life with them" relevant. Now people were free to jump from bed to bed with little thought to the consequences because most of the consequences were seemingly eliminated. Nearly thirty years down the road, I believe we are seeing the results of this decision. The family is crumbling. Young criminals are getting younger without the influence of fathers in the home. Sex without consequences as the world sees it, is leaving people hurt and broken all over the place. The medical profession has been corrupted to the point that Doctors, who are among our nation's best and brightest, see nothing wrong with the infanticide called partial birth abortion.

Seventy-five percent of the people in our prisons today are there because of drugs and drug related offenses. Why are drugs running so rampant in our society? I believe it has to do with two factors. One is that even in the most prosperous nation in the world, many people are leading empty lives. There is something missing in their lives, and they don't know what it is. Eventually they get to the point where the only thing they can do is "medicate". And once they are hooked, they will do anything to get more "medication". The other group sees the need of the addict as a path to great wealth. They take advantage of the opportunity, putting their lives in great peril in exchange for a whole lot of money.

Why have I told all these stories in a book about being an authentic Christian? The answer can be found in the first commandment. "I am the Lord thy God thou shalt have no other gods before me." In America today, we think that if we are not bowing down before a statue, we are not worshipping false gods. Nothing could be further from the truth. Jesus said, "Where your treasure is, there is your heart". Anything that you put before God can very quickly become a god to you. In America, as throughout the world, the worship of the almighty dollar is evident. We are willing to excuse immorality in the highest offices as long as we have money and prosperity. Even as the consequences begin to rear their ugly heads, we roll around fat and happy and oblivious to them because we have a few dollars in our pocket. Why should we worry about immorality when our "gods" are being well served?

We are willing to endure long hours at the office and weeks and weeks on the road away from our families, so that we can give them more things, when what they really need is us in the home. This perpetuates the cycle of placing possessions and money before what is really important, until eventually our kids are even more materialistic than we are. The evidence around us shows us this is causing destruction, but we are too busy serving our "god" to notice.

Abortion shows us a few more false "gods." Once again, the financial aspect comes into play. Babies severely cut into our ability to earn money, so we sacrifice them to our "gods." Babies are also inconvenient at times, so we lay them on the altar of our "god" called "convenience." Most importantly, babies are a consequence of having sex with whomever we feel like, whenever we feel like it. "Why should there be consequences to something that feels so good, and besides I have a right..." and so we lay our children on the altar of the "god" called "self".

By doing this, we feel we have absolved ourselves of all consequence, and yet the consequences are running rampant all around us. People are no longer holding life as sacred. Further, through the attitude that no action should have a consequence, illegitimacy has gone through the roof leaving fatherless children with mothers who can't control them. Men have stopped stepping up to the plate and doing their duty to take care of the children they make and women have abdicated the responsibility of checking to see if a man will stick around, marry them and support his family.

The drug problem shows us the "gods" of "self" and "money" run amok. On the demand side are the users. People willing to risk their lives for a feeling, a "high," if you will, are totally sold out to the "god" of "self." As their addiction progresses, eventually they get to the point where it is their self that they lay on the altar. Willing to endure anything, no matter how vile, willing to victimize, lie, cheat and steal and finally sometimes willing to die, their lives a sacrifice to the "god of self." The "dealers" make up the supply side. "Self, money and power" are their "gods" and eventually they end up sacrificing themselves, with crime, imprisonment and even death as their reward.

Is there any hope? Yes, because, as usual, God (the only true God) has a better way. An answer that hurting people are looking for, is right in front of their eyes and Radically Real Christians have got to be ready to tell them about it. Jesus tells us to lay up our treasures in heaven. He is telling us to work for the things that really matter, to make serving Him our purpose in life. To do what we do for the reward He has to offer. To give what we cannot keep (our lives), to gain what we cannot lose (eternal life). Makes sense to me! A life of serving God is more fulfilling than anything the world has to offer.

Now I know what you are thinking, it will be a tough sale. But friends this is not for sale, God's gift is free. Our job is to show the people who are seeking purpose the way. You really won't have to look too far to find people seeking purpose. They are everywhere. They are in the rat race losing to the rats. They are wealthy people who are constantly seeking more because they find that wealth is not filling their lives. They are people who are chasing from person to person, partner to partner trying to find the person to complete their lives. They are kids whose parents are too busy chasing money. They are parents whose kids are out of control, chasing after the world. They are your friends, your neighbors, your family and they are crying out for something to fill the void. Rejoice! Radically Real Christian you have been blessed with exactly what they need to fill the void, the saving love of Jesus Christ. Show that to them from your life and the Spirit working through you WILL win them to Christ.

But before you go forward, you have to check yourself out. Do you have any false gods in your life? Remember authenticity is the key. So, let's take a minute and check ourselves to see if we are Radically Real.

Is It an Idol?

The first thing you might be thinking is that you don't have any of the false gods listed above. If that is the case, great, but that's not all there is to it. You see anything that comes between you and God is an idol. Remember, where your treasure is there is your heart. Where is your treasure? What do you value the most? What is your number one priority? Don't just give me the Sunday School answer, really examine your life. And don't make the mistake of thinking well that's harmless enough, isn't it? Remember what God said, "Thou shalt have NO other gods before me." If it is coming before God in your life, you need to change that if you want to be Radically Real.

Let's look at a few together:

Family--I put the tough one first. "How can family be a false god?" you ask. If it comes before God, your family can be a god. Now rest assured, I am pretty sure that God wants this to be a very near second to Him. The love of our family should be second only to God. Our family, after all, is one of His great blessings. But look at what God did with His own son!

Look at Abraham, who at 100 years old had his first son. What did God ask of him? As a test to see if he was still number one in Abraham's life, He asked Abraham to sacrifice the very son God promised him. (We will cover this in detail in a few pages, stay tuned.) I'm not saying that God will ever ask you to sacrifice your children, physically, but there may be a time when you have to be away from them to serve Him. One of the things we have to do is trust the Lord to care for our families while we are away. We also have to be in prayer that we will not go the opposite direction and make a "god' out of our ministry and sacrifice our family to it.

The other side of it is that there have been people that have been led away from Christ out of devotion to their families. This is not right. Radically Real Christians are called to be a light to the world, that includes our families, and we must speak the truth in love, pray for them and lead them to Christ.

What good are we to our families if we do not reach out to them with the love of Jesus Christ? Our first witness is to our family. They are our first "mission field". The family should be a priority, but they must come second to God. The good news is that if we give ourselves completely to God, He will make us the best we can possibly be. In that way, we will be better for our families than we could ever be on our own.

Sports and Hobbies--"How harmless can that be?" you ask. Does your Sunday morning golf game keep you from church? And before you say, I can worship God anywhere even on the golf course, I will remind you of two things: 1. Let us not give up meeting together--Hebrews 10:25 and 2. When you hit your fifth ball into the sand trap is your attitude really one of worship? Do you miss your Wednesday Bible study, to go to Softball practice? Do you sleep through church because you were up too late the night before at your bowling league? If this is the case, is God really first in your life? We start this attitude off early when we allow our children to participate in sports activities instead of being at worship. I know what you're thinking, "But the kids have to play in the tournament or they will be off the team." There are two things to consider here. The first is this, if every parent claiming to be a Christian, kept their kid home on Sunday, would the sports leagues not soon be forced to not hold games on Sunday or at least until after the worship hour? The second is this, which is more important, God or playing little league. Serving God must be first!

This might be a great opportunity to be Radically Real. If your interest is in sports, use it for God. Start a league that plays at times other than worship times. Have a golf outing where believers are encouraged to take their friends out in foursomes and witness, just don't do it on Sunday morning!

Career--Yes you have to work, yes you have to earn a living, but what position in your life does your career occupy? Do you work all day and all night trying to get ahead? Are you running yourself in to the ground to try to be number one? Does your family need a photo of you to remember what you look like? Are you working harder and harder to give your family more and more things and finding them to be more and more ungrateful? They may need less things and more you.

I fell into this trap. For a long time, I felt I was wanted to be a famous artist. I worked day and night. I put it before my family, my church, God and even my own physical needs. I worked as much as 20 hours a day. I figured, "I have a God given talent, and I am working very hard, God has to bless me." I rationalized that my family would benefit when I "made it". I was wrong on all counts. God did not bless my efforts. I had made a God of my work. My relationship with my son had disintegrated to the point where we hardly talked. (I am still working hard to rebuild it years later.) I even nearly lost my marriage. All because I was determined to make this career of mine to succeed. I praise God that he turned me around. When I gave my life to Christ, I made a mistake. I didn't give it all to Him. I held my career back. Trying to run that one aspect of my life nearly ruined me. When the devil saw me holding on to that one thing, he knew right where to hit me and it hurt, bad. Learn from my stupidity. A career makes a lousy god. Accept no substitutes. What you do for a living is not nearly as important as what God does for you.

That Special Someone--Yes, he or she can become a god. Build your relationship on Christ. Dating is an audition for marriage, treat the relationship accordingly. Make sure that the other person is also seeking to be Radically Real. Being evenly yoked, means being married to someone of like faith. Do not make the mistake of believing that you will change someone, only God can do that. Do not let anyone lead you away from your faith. Remember, you are supposed to be salt and light. The best gift of love you can give is the gift of Jesus.

And of course, sex outside of marriage, will complicate your life and damage your witness and there is no room for that in the life of a person that is seeking to be Radically Real. Your mission from God is to be Radically Real. If you put someone before God, they become your god.

Money and Possessions--Yes even the person seeking to be Radically Real can get caught in that trap. We all need money and contrary to popular belief money is not the root of all evil. The love of money is the root of all evil. God has promised to provide for all our needs. He also tells us we need to work. Just seek His Kingdom first and He will give you what you need. Radically Real people do their best and let God be God. What He blesses us with is still His and He gives it to be used for His glory, treat your money and possessions that way and amazing things will happen. People will see your good works and want to know why you are so generous. What a great way to witness. What a great way to be Radically Real!

Talents--Talents are a gift from God. He never promised to make us rich in what the world has to offer with them. If we are using them for our own glory, we are misusing them and selling God short. Telling Him that His rewards are not worth waiting for, when His are worth so much more than what this world has to offer. Our talents like everything else He gives us are to be for His glory. If we use them that way, we cannot help but be blessed.

Ministry--Every Christian is called to a ministry of one kind or another. How can ministry become a God? If we become self-motivated, and use it to grab glory for ourselves, rather than glorify God. Our purpose is to glorify God and Him only. Personal glory is not Radically Real. The reward for ministry is eternal and in Heaven. If we minister to give glory to ourselves, we gain a shallow reward that will fade away. That's not enough of a reward for a Radically Real Christian.

Radically Real Christians store their treasure in heaven.

This is by no means a comprehensive list. There are countless thousands of things that can, given the opportunity, become false gods. The test remains the same. Step one is to pray to God to ask Him to reveal areas that are coming before Him in your life. If you have a doubt as to whether or not something is becoming a god in your life, give it the first commandment test.

Very simply, ask yourself this question, "Is my commitment to ________ greater than my commitment to God?" Then ask, "If I asked ________ (a friend, neighbor or family member) if my commitment to ______ is greater than my commitment to God, what would they say?" If it passes both of these tests, it is not a false god. (Although, if you had to ask there is a good chance, you are at least in danger of making it a false god, so be careful.) If it does not, you know what you need to do, get on your knees and pray, ask God to forgive you. Ask Him to help you gain perspective and put this thing in its proper place.

For me, when I became convicted that my art career was becoming a god to me, I had to leave it behind. I gave up most of my artwork for a while. Eventually God gave it back to me. Now I use my talent to His glory as a part of my ministry. As long as it occupies its proper place in my life, it is OK to use it. As a matter of fact, it is expected that I use this God-given ability as the Spirit leads.

ONE WORD OF CAUTION--One of the possible false gods I have listed is family. Let it never be said that anyone has ever left his/her family because of what I have written. That would be a misinterpretation of what I have written. The Scriptures are full of guidelines for parents. Proverbs is a great place to start. Ask God to guide you and help you to keep perspective. A wife is called to submit to her husband. A husband is called to love his wife like Christ loved the church. Family unity is key to being all that God has called us to be. It is key to being Radically Real.

Now that you have given your life a thorough examination, (if you haven't done it, get your bookmark, mark your page and close the book and do it now. This is not a novel; it is a book that is meant to make you make changes.) it is time to take it to the world. People are looking for answers. Ask God to show you people you can help and reach out to.

Filling The God Shaped Hole

The God-shaped hole is that space in your life that you struggled to fill. Everyone has one. It is a place in your heart that only God can fill; nothing else will do it. People speak of an internal emptiness or a void in their lives. It is something that drives people to do outrageous things just to fill the void. Why do we have it? It is what makes us seek God. The few people that find God and His grace through Jesus Christ find a peace of having their God-shaped hole filled. Once we find this answer, we cannot be Radically Real if we do not share it with all who will listen. The following are symptoms of the problem. People that exhibit these symptoms whether they believe it or not are seeking God in their lives. Some will adamantly refuse to believe it, but Radically Real Christians are not easily discouraged. We are only called to shine the light. When we do it, God will in His timing show them the way.

Money--We all know them, they have everything the world has to offer and still they want more. This goes far beyond mere greed. They are trying to fill a hole in their life the size of the infinite Creator of the universe. Nothing is ever enough. They will do whatever it takes to get more and fill the void; acquisition becomes the answer they pursue. The biggest house, the best schools, the hottest cars, the newest toys and whatever else they can think of--they have to have 'em. "Maybe just one more thing will do it, no not quite, maybe if I have that, no that's not it either." It is hard to see their lives and think of them as having a void, since often we covet what they have. That is why that "thou shalt not covet" commandment is among the ten. All that money and all those possessions just bring emptiness.

How to reach the money, obsessed person: First of all, as with everything else, the first step is always to seek the Lord. Ask Him how to reach out. The following are suggestions arrived at after my own prayer. First, no matter what, wipe all envy from your mind. You have a storehouse of treasures in Heaven that will dwarf anything this world has to offer. Second, show this person your joy. That is what they are looking for. Make them wonder and then let them know why you are happy. Let them know where your hope comes from. Always be sincere. Never put up a front. When you are facing a trial, remember that joy will come with the morning. Three, don't hit them up for a donation, don't ask them for anything! Their self-esteem comes from their acquisitions. They have all kinds of people that want something from them. You want to be different. You (through Christ) are the one doing the giving. What you have to offer cannot be bought.

The person who sees money as the way to fill their void may also be led to assume that because they have great wealth that they have no need of God, or they may assume that their wealth is a sign that they are blessed and OK with God. Neither of these is true. Every person needs God.

Every person needs a saving relationship with Jesus Christ (John 14:6). This person may be difficult to reach. Human nature is that we rarely feel the need for God when things are going well. Trust God, pray and keep showing that person your joy and they will start to wonder why you are so happy. Then be prepared to help them find their way to Christ.

Career--Career is similar to money in that they can seem to go hand in hand. The career-oriented person tries to fill the void with success, promotions, titles, corner offices, self-employment, etc. There is nothing wrong with any of these things, but the person that is using career to fill his God-shaped hole is obsessed with them. They are the ones that will do whatever it takes. They will put their family behind their career, their God and their church, if they have time for either one. They are the ones that are always working, always striving, always finding excuses to do more. They have crossed over the line from motivated to work-a-holics. The person who tries to fill his void with his career's family needs a picture of him so they remember what he looks like. This person rationalizes that they are doing all this work to benefit their family, but if they want to be totally honest, they carry a lot of guilt.

How to reach the career obsessed person: Ask God to show you the right way and then: First, show them your priorities, this may mean, you give up the promotion and the raise to spend more time with your family. Always temper this with the fact that your family will only exist as it does now for a short period of time and it is more important to you than your career to be involved. Never, repeat never, play the guilt game. Never slam them for their choices. This will only cause defensiveness. You simply want to show them by example that your choice is the better way. Remember the Sabbath; always take one day a week for the Lord. Carve this in stone. If you are asked why, explain why the Lord is so important to you. Do this factually, without moral superiority. Instead, explain to them what the benefits of worship are to you. Lastly, do all that you can to be a good example. In your allotted working time, be the best you can be. Work as hard as you can. Help people cheerfully and always be the epitome of positive morale. Be completely honest! Be impressive to all those around you and give God the glory. In short be Radically Real.

Talent--Again, similar to career. These people seek a new dimension. Besides money and prestige, these people become obsessed with the adoration of other people, fame. They are willing to do almost anything to "make it" in their profession. Anything "less" than success in their field is totally unacceptable. They would rather starve than do a "menial" job. Pride becomes a major issue. They crave attention at the expense of all else.

The problem they will run into is that fame and popularity are very fleeting. Styles and fads change. Even if they find a certain degree of success, there is a good chance that they could become the "flavor of the month," quickly passed by for something or someone else. An example of this would be the "one hit wonder," a musician or performer that comes from nowhere and soars to the top of the charts, only to be forgotten. They get what Andy Warhol called 15 minutes of fame. They then spend the rest of their lives trying to recapture past glory.

The other danger comes with success. Remember only God can fill the God-shaped hole. The person finds their fame is not enough to fill the hole and so they continue to work harder and harder to acquire more and more until they become a parody of themselves. Or they try to compensate by excessive living, spending themselves into bankruptcy, drinking and drugging themselves into oblivion, or jumping from relationship to relationship. None of these will work.

How to reach the talent obsessed person: Ask God to show you the way. Then get to know them. Be their friend. If they have fame, don't fall all over them, give them respect but treat them as an equal. They already have enough people willing to fall all over them. They need someone to be real with them. Show them the difference that Christ has made in your life. Show them the way Christ has made your life full. Try to show them how God could use their talent to make a real difference in the world. That is the reason God chose to bless them with that talent to begin with.

Power--How many times have you heard it? Absolute power corrupts absolutely. The person obsessed with power is trying to be his or her own god. They are always seeking more and more power. Their task is the hardest of all, trying to fill their God-shaped hole with their own importance. To them, people are an expendable commodity to be used for their gain and God is just someone competing for their power. Pride is their guiding force in life. Emptiness is a by-product of their obsession. They always want more and more power and they will sacrifice anything to get it.

How to reach the power obsessed person: Ask God to show you the way to reach this person. (I know I keep repeating that but it is the key!) This task will be difficult, because the power obsessed person by nature is trying to be his own god. The need for god in their own life may not seem apparent to him especially if things are going well. The key is to show them that you have peace of mind in Christ. Peace of mind is usually lacking in a person that is always trying to climb higher and grab more. Being your own god is hard work. Show this person your respect for others and the importance of relationships in your life. Model for them the love of Jesus. Don't be surprised if this person finds your way of life foolish. A sense of superiority often comes with a lot of power. The powerful people of Jesus' day thought He was foolish too, but in the end He won.

Possessions--The one who dies with the most toys wins, is the attitude of the person trying to fill their God-shaped hole with possessions. Similar in attitude to the person obsessed with money, this person always just wants more and more and more. The big bank account is not the important thing here. As a matter of fact, these people will often spend themselves into bankruptcy trying to fill their void. Pride and obsession over things can come to no good. People in their lives will begin to see that they cannot hope to measure up to their "precious stuff". The Lord tells us flat out that things cannot help but let us down. Things that can rust, that moths can eat, things that can burn and be stolen will never fill the God-shaped hole. When something happens to one of our things, we become obsessed with getting something bigger and better. God has promised to meet our physical needs. Becoming obsessed by possessions rejects God's ability to provide what we need.

People sometimes have a hard time believing they are obsessed with things. They rationalize that the things are all things that they need. They rationalize that they need a house to live in and they are right, but they go out and buy a house that requires them to work 70 hours a week to pay for. Their every thought is in paying for and finding the time to maintain their property. They rationalize that they need a car to get back and forth to work. For the most part they are right, but they go out and buy a car that is so expensive that they can't afford to repair it when it breaks and they all break sooner or later. If you spend the Sunday morning worship time polishing your car or mowing your yard, look at what you are working on. You are now looking at your god.

How to reach the person obsessed with possessions: First ask God for guidance on how to reach out to them. 1. Then show them the peace you have by living within your means. If you are not living within your means, now is the time to start. Remember, sometimes being Radically Real means removing the plank from our own eye before we help our neighbor with their speck. Most of us have debt. The trend toward debt free living is the way to go, but to be honest, I haven't figured out how to do it yet, but what I have done is made a real effort to keep my debt to a minimum, and that is one thing we all can do. 2. Show them what holds real importance in your life. Show them the things in your life that hold value to you: your family, time with friends, nature, and most importantly your time with God. Model for them a life where things are truly in perspective as the blessings God has given to be used to serve him and meet our needs.

People--How can people become a god? When we try to use them to fill the space that only God can fill. When you think about it, it is really a lot to ask of a person to fill the space of God. People are not perfect and will eventually hurt us or let us down. People obsessed with people are basically people that allow their friends to drag them down. They are extremely susceptible to peer pressure. They will do almost anything to maintain a friendship, even things that are stupid, dangerous or illegal. Fitting in means everything to these people, no matter what crowd they are in. A lot of times, people that fall into this trap are people that have a hard time being accepted.

There is one place that people should always find acceptance and that is the church. God loves us just the way we are, but he loves us too much to let us stay that way.

How to reach the person obsessed with fitting in: Ask God how to reach this person, then: 1. Befriend this person and show them the importance of God in your life. Show them the difference Jesus makes. Once you have established that you are a true friend to them, begin to show them how others are dragging them down. You might even try establishing a little "positive peer pressure". IMPORTANT: This is not manipulation. You must be a true friend. You don't just get the result you are looking for and then move on. If you can't be a true friend, find someone who can. This person is looking for people they can depend on through thick and thin. If you have a hit and run friendship, they will feel betrayed by not only you, but also the God you serve. And that is definitely not Radically Real. The point is we want to show this person that only God is totally dependable, but that in Christ we are willing to strive to be the best, most supportive friend possible. You can't do that insincerely, and it is only really possible through the love of Christ.

Sex--This can manifest itself in a number of ways. From the person who will give themselves to anyone in the hopes of finding someone who will fill the void in their life to the person, on a "power trip" stacking up conquests in an effort to fill their own emptiness. While both are ultimately self-destructive, it is the latter that wreaks havoc on people all around them and ultimately, often creates more of the former.

The difference in the two types is quite simple, the first person is looking for love and the second is looking for power. For too long, we have been victim of a ludicrous term: "making love." Sex does not make love. Sex is a result of love. In any other way it is an animal function. Most people don't see it that way, but that does not change the factuality of the statement. Sex was designed by God; for use in a loving, lifetime, marriage commitment. It has been corrupted by the enemy to the point of being nothing but pure physical pleasure. One need only look at our society to see that this is true. Thirty million plus abortions, STD's, prostitution, 50 percent plus divorce rate are all the symptoms of sex having perverted into something it was never intended to be.

How to reach out to a sex obsessed world--First ask God how to proceed. Radically Real Christians need to show a better way. We need to remain committed to our marriages. We need to forego sex before marriage and hold out for the person that God has made for us. The world glorifies the other side of sex but consistently fails to show the consequences. We know better, and as we begin to show what we know, as strange as this may seem, it will appeal to those who have been hurt time and time again. We have the right way, no matter what the world says. If we are true to God, people will notice.

Now I know, some of you are thinking it's too late for me, I have already messed up. That is the beauty of what Jesus has done for us. All have sinned and fallen short of the glory of God. The good news is like the woman caught in adultery, (Luke 7) we can "go and sin no more." We can repent and move forward, and that is exactly what we need to do. It is never easy for those of us with a past to show the world a better way, but with God all things are possible. Share the pain of your wrong decisions and show how life is better this way. It is always OK to share your struggles, just make sure you remember to also share your victory.

The Most Excellent Way--All of this really comes down to one thing, which will be a consistent theme throughout this book. The key is letting your light shine. The key is showing people that there is only one God and that everything else in life is a gift from Him. Used properly (to His glory) they are great blessings that can bring us joy. Used improperly, they can be an unending source of pain. Regardless of how it is received we are obligated to "speak the truth in love." I truly believe that if we present this truth in "the most excellent way" (love, 1 Corinthians 13) that people will see the light of the Lord and gravitate toward Him. One thing to remember, you are not guaranteed to see the results of the efforts you have made, some sow the seed, some water and God brings the increase. Just because you do not see the change doesn't mean there is none. God is in control. All you have to do is what he tells you.

Radically Real People from the Bible

Abraham

When it comes to people who had their treasures in the right place in the Bible, few people can compare to Abraham. Abraham went where God told him to go and did what God told him to do. He was not a perfect person (only Jesus pulled that off) but we can draw many things from the story of God's servant Abraham.

You see Abram was doing pretty well. He had many things, and he had a very loving wife but there was something missing. He didn't have any children. His wife Sarai was unable to conceive. One night, God spoke to Abram and told him that he would be the father of a great nation, that his descendants would outnumber the stars in the sky.

But there was a problem with this, Abram, whose name had been changed to Abraham by God at this revelation, was nearing 90 years old. His wife Sarah (her name had changed too) was creeping up on 80. At this point, they still had no kids. As someone who's pushing 40 and can't imagine another baby at this age, my mind is boggled, but this is God we are talking about and with Him all things are possible.

Now of course, there is a caution with this, Abraham and Sarah grew impatient waiting on God. In fairness to them they were pretty old. Why, even at this point, Abraham would have be 108 years old when the kid graduated. But, because they grew impatient, they made their own plan, Sarah would give Abraham Hagar, her servant, as a wife so that she could have children for Sarah. Never make your own plan, especially when God has already told you His. Seek His plan, it is perfect. The result of Abraham's union with Hagar was Ishmael, and his descendants have been In dispute with the descendants of Abraham virtually ever since. When we don't follow God's plan it can lead to disaster. God works on His own schedule. It is His privilege. He is God after all. Sometimes we have to wait for Him, but don't worry, He is working hard to prepare you to complete the mission He has laid out for you.

Back to our story. When Abraham is 100 years old and Sarah is 90, she finally gives birth to a son, who she named Isaac. God had fulfilled his promise to Abraham. Through Isaac, the nation of Israel would be born. Abraham loved his son Isaac very much. God wanted to show Abraham something very important. He tested Abraham to show that although His son was very important that God must be supreme in his life. He asked Abraham to sacrifice his son on the altar. The son Abraham had waited for, for 100 years. Imagine it, after 100 years of waiting, Abraham had a son and now God was asking him to kill him as a sacrifice. What a test! But you know what? Abraham passed. You see his faith was great in the promises of the Lord. Hebrews 11 tells us that Abraham believed that God could raise the dead. What's important here for us to remember is this. At this point, there is no New Testament. At this point there is no story of Lazarus. There has been no resurrection of Jesus and there won't be one for 3000 or so years. No, Abraham just simply put all his faith in God. He went about the task of doing what God asked.

Can you picture what was going on inside him as he and his son made their way up the mountain? You can imagine that the devil was hitting him with double barrel blasts of doubt. "Did God really tell you to do this?" "What if Isaac stays dead?" "You will be a murderer!" "Sarah will kill you!" "Just look at this 'Great God' you serve that would make you wait 100 years for a kid and then ask you to kill Him." "Is it worth it?" But Abraham persevered. Abraham ultimately trusted God.

Can you imagine how Abraham's heart broke when young Isaac asked, "Father, where is the lamb?" But Abraham's answer shows his faith is still secure, "The Lord himself will provide the lamb." I can imagine the way Abraham felt as he laid his son, his long-awaited son on the altar. I can imagine the fervent prayers going up as Abraham raised the knife. And, most importantly, I can imagine the immense relief as the Angel of the Lord showed Abraham the ram in the thicket that would take Isaac's place on the altar. Abraham had passed the test. Could you?

See God, in His wisdom and mercy gave Abraham a substitute. He gave that ram and allowed Abraham to keep his son. God now knew beyond the shadow of a doubt that although Abraham treasured his son, that he treasured God all the more. Abraham's treasure was in the right place. Eventually, God would sacrifice His own son for the children of Abraham and all the other children who would accept Him and store up their treasures in heaven. What God allowed Abraham to do by keeping back his son, He did not allow Himself. And that perfect Sacrifice of Jesus is our hope of eternal life.

As I write the story of Abraham, I must admit I am concerned. You see I know that someone out there reading this book might misunderstand. That someone, misguided might do harm to a child. God is not in the sacrifices business anymore, at least not the physical, animal burnt offering kind. Jesus covered that. When He gave his life on that cross, He became our sacrifice, and if we accept Him and repent, we can be right with God. If you would even think of harming your child, get help, talk to someone. Pray that God would show you a better way. While we may have to sacrifice some time with our children to serve the kingdom of God, the kind of sacrifice Abraham was called to make will never be asked again. Jesus paid it all!

Chapter 11

Coming Out of the (Prayer) Closet

Living as a Christian Out in the Open

I tell you, whoever acknowledges me before men, the Son of Man will also acknowledge him before the angels of God. But he who disowns me before men will be disowned before the angels of God. And everyone who speaks against the son of man will be forgiven, but anyone who blasphemes against the Holy Spirit will not be forgiven.

--Luke 12: 8-10

Why do we act as though we are ashamed of our faith? Now I know that this is a bold statement and if it doesn't apply to you, great, you are well on your way to being Radically Real, but we can see by the falling away from many denominations that something is very clearly wrong.

I believe the problem is starting from a false tolerance. In the old days, tolerance meant something to the effect that you could disagree with someone and yet not feel the need to beat them with a claw hammer. Tolerance is a good thing. We should be loving, and caring. We should model Jesus' character. We should meet people where they are. This is true tolerance.

The "tolerance" I am speaking of now is not that kind of tolerance. The tolerance I am talking about is the tolerance that says that the only thing that is wrong is saying something is wrong. It is a tolerance without standards, or at least not biblical ones. Today tolerance means that there are no absolute truths. Christianity is a faith that is based on the absolute truth of Jesus Christ. In John 14: 6 Jesus says, very clearly, I am the truth. In John chapter 8, Jesus tells us that the truth will set us free. If we Christians are reluctant to share the truth, or worse yet, believe the truth, our faith becomes irrelevant.

I believe that that is exactly what we are seeing today. Christians are allowing Christianity to become just another irrelevant faith. Radically Real Christians, I am sounding the battle cry. It is time for us to come out of the prayer closet! It is time to show the world that our faith is not only relevant, but the only true faith. Jesus Christ is the only way to Heaven. If you don't believe that you don't have a hope in...well let's just say under Heaven, of ever being Radically Real. Close this book, fall to your knees and pray until you believe it and then rejoin us.

If that last part sounded a bit harsh, forgive me but it is the truth and we have got to stop compromising on the truth. Am I calling for hatred? No! Am I calling for us to lash out against non-Christians? Of course not! I am calling Christians to return to believing in Biblical Christianity, of being unashamed of the Gospel and of going into the world with a real and relevant faith that the lost people of this world will be drawn to like moths to a light.

The silence of the church is allowing this world to crumble under the weight of sin. It is time to stop wringing our hands and stop lamenting the decay of our society. That is like a doctor discovering the cure for cancer and then throwing it away and crying over the rampaging effects of the disease. This world is sick and we have the cure in our hands. The disease is sin and the cure is Jesus. For too long, the church has been sitting on the cure. It is time to make a change.

One of my favorite parables of Jesus is the parable of the talents. In it a master gives three servants money (talents) to invest while he is gone. He gives them each an amount that is dependent on his ability. The first two take what they have been given and invest wisely. They double his money and when the master returns, He is well pleased. The third guy is a worry wart. He takes the money and buries it in the ground so that the master will not suffer a loss. When the master returns, he gives him back the original sum. You know the story. The master is so angry, that he takes what was given to the man and gives it to the servant who made the greatest gain.

Where are we in that picture? Can you see the writing on the wall? The signs in the Bible are being fulfilled more and more every day. The Master is on His way back. When he comes what will He say to you? Have you invested what He has given you well, or have you buried it in the backyard? Afraid to take a chance, to take a risk, have you wasted your opportunity to serve the master? He has not returned yet, so you still have time but it is time to get moving. 1 Peter 4:10 tells us that each of us must use whatever gifts he has received to serve others. What have you done with what you have been given?

If someone were to ask me what the number one enemy of the church today was, well I guess I would have to say Satan is number one, let's not kid ourselves. Number two however, to my mind, beyond the shadow of a doubt, is the comfort zone. The comfort zone is that little place where we feel all comfy and cozy and secure. Everybody has a comfort zone, but let me say it again, I believe that the comfort zone is the enemy of the church.

You see there are essentially two spheres of human existence, the church and the world. The church is made up of the body of Christ, the people who have accepted Jesus Christ as Lord and Savior. The world is made up of, well, everybody else. Now there may be some people who bristle at that analogy but what do we believe? We believe that Jesus said, "I am the Way and the Truth and the Life no man comes to the Father except through me." (John 14:6 NIV) Any other way of stating it for the Radically Real Christian is nothing but politically correct "waffling" that serves no purpose except to keep people out of Heaven and make us look tolerant to the perishing. What are we sneaking around for?

You see, church, we have a mission to complete. We are on a mission from God. Our mission is to leave the sphere called the church, go into the sphere called the world and bring people to the sphere of the church, which is not the physical building so much as it is the body of Christ. Where we run into the problem is that the church is a very comfortable place. We are with people who believe like us. We have our squabbles at times but essentially everyone there is of the mindset that Jesus is Lord and we are seeking to follow Him. The church becomes our sanctuary from the world. That is OK and even great for a while, but we can't stay there. We are instructed to go to the other sphere.

Now the other sphere can be a dark place and it can be a lonely place for the Radically Real Christian. The people there don't believe like us, as a matter of fact many of them believe that our beliefs are bigoted and wrong. We may find ourselves put down and ridiculed in the other sphere.

Even worse things may happen, you see another guy is in charge of the other sphere and the people out there are captive to his mind set. The world is so scary to some in the church that they never really go there and the church becomes a comfort zone. But there is a big problem with this. Think about the most famous verse in the scriptures, John 3:16. What does Jesus say here? He says, "for God so loved the world." God loves the world. How much? Enough to die for them, that's how much. We are also instructed to be in the world but not of the world. We need to be in the world if we are going to tell the world.

Let's get one thing straight right now. I said it before and I'll say it again, the church is not a country club for saints, the church is a hospital for sinners. It is a triage center for people to be patched up, healed and sent back to the frontlines and the battle. The battle is not against the world, the battle is against the enemy himself. The good news is that we are assured of victory. Jesus has already won the war. All we have to do is be faithful to Him.

It is time for the church to leave the comfort zone. If your church is too comfortable, change it. We are not supposed to stay there. We are not supposed to live there. We are supposed to go out and bring people in. People that may not look like us, people that may not dress like us, people that come from different backgrounds, people that drink and use drugs and smoke, people that may not know how to act in church, people that have piercings and tattoos, you know, sinners just like us. We have got to lose the mind-set that we are in the church because we are worthy but somehow those on the outside are not. All have sinned and fallen short of the glory of God. We are instructed to bring people just as they are to meet Jesus.

We need to stop feeling like people need to clean up somehow to come to Christ. Jesus wants them to be part of His family just like He wants you. He will help them deal with what He wants to change in His life. Remember, Romans 5: 8, "But God demonstrates His own love for us in this: While we were yet sinners, Christ died for us." The implication is quite clear, Jesus loves us so much that He died for us and He died for them too. They are not strangers, they are not the enemy, they are brothers and sisters who got lost along the way. It is up to us to help them find their way home, but we can't do that if we don't go where they are.

Remember, the church is supposed to be a hospital for sinners. Do you ever really feel comfortable in a hospital? No, there is a tension there. There is always someone rolling in who needs the help of a doctor, always someone that needs something. That's how are churches should be. The church should be a place where people are constantly becoming aware of the need for the savior. It should also be a place where the church, that is the body of Christ, becomes keenly aware of its own need for healing. We should never forget that we are sinners saved by grace. This helps us to have compassion on the folks all around us. We are no more deserving of God's grace than they are.

How dare we ever think that a person deserves a certain consequence as if we are any less deserving of the consequences of our sin? Sin is sin, and we must never fool ourselves into believing that our sins are any less bad than anyone else's. We are not called to make those judgments anyway. We are like ambulance drivers bringing the sick and injured to the Great Physician. An ambulance driver would never stand over someone who had been injured and say, "you idiot, why did you go and do that"? It's not his job, his job is to get the person to the doctor. The doctor will make the judgment on the person's condition and tell the person how not to get hurt again. That is His job.

As we look at the scripture that started this chapter there are a few things to consider. Jesus tells us that whoever acknowledges Him before men, He will acknowledge before His Father in Heaven. My question is, "How can we acknowledge Jesus before men, if we are never before men that need to hear about Him"? You see, I believe that we need to acknowledge Him before the lost and the found. I believe that we better take every opportunity to share Him. God will provide the opportunities and if we don't take them, are we really acknowledging Him at all? It is easy to acknowledge Him before other believers. Where the rubber meets the road is when we acknowledge Him before the non-believer. Also, how can we acknowledge Him before men if we are not transparent about what He has done in our lives? In other words, can we acknowledge the difference Jesus has made in our lives, if we are not out in the open about our past sin and even our struggles today? Isn't that part of acknowledging Jesus?

It's this simple really, going back to the hospital analogy. Suppose you have a serious disease, a fatal disease, like cancer. Suppose your prognosis is terminal, you are going to die. In a last-ditch effort, you are referred to a doctor, who treats you and cures you and gives you a new lease on life. What would you do for him? You'd write letters to the editor, put up a sign, go on TV, tell everyone you know about Him and seek out anyone that had that disease and refer them to this miraculous healer. You'd do that, wouldn't you? Well, you have that disease, you have a disease with a 100% mortality rate. It's called sin and rather than just a physical death, sin causes eternal death. The Bible tells us that the wages of sin is death. It is inescapable, but there is good news, if you are a Christian, even though, unless the Lord returns, your physical body will die, you have been cured. The verse finishes with "but the gift of God is eternal life in Christ Jesus our Lord." You have a new lease on life thanks to the Great Physician, Jesus Christ. Who are you going to tell? You see, a lot of the people that you know and love are still infected. The symptoms are visible but they are always attributed to something else and a lot of times people don't realize they are infected with sin until it's too late. You have the cure in your hands, all you have to do is share it. Will you?

The Lord has called us to go into the world, (we will discuss this in much greater detail in the next chapter). We must do what He has called us to do if we want to be Radically Real. Let's look at what we need to do as we come out of the prayer closet and reach out with the love of Jesus.

They Don't Care How Much You Know...

We all know the old saying, "They don't care how much you know 'til they know how much you care. It is so true. You cannot just go up to someone and yell, "sinner, get saved." Oh, it may be the truth, (OK, it is the truth) but will they listen? No, they will not. They will clam up, or worse and you may never get the opportunity to share with them again. So how do you share Christ with someone without driving them away? In a lot of cases the answer is relationally. In other words, you show people that you care. The first step in this is the same as the first step in almost every Christian undertaking, prayer. Ask God to give you the opportunity to share His love. Ask Him to give you the right words. You may not always have a lot of time to pray this prayer but that's OK, God can listen fast and since He already knows what we need before we ask, He is ready to help. Then be real. Be in the open. Don't just slap a tract in their hand and leave, tell them the truth. Take the time to care.

The truth of the matter is that you may be the only Jesus some people ever meet. To tell the truth, with most people the most important thing we can do to show we care, is to listen. Resist the temptation to correct them. Let them say what is on their mind. Never get argumentative. Trust that God will give you a time to speak your piece. After they have shared, or gotten it off their chest, whichever the case may be, it's your turn.

Let Them Know What God Has Done For You

Don't come off high and mighty. Tell the truth, the whole truth and nothing but the truth. Contrary to popular belief there is only one truth. That is the one you need to share. Don't gloss over it. You have to be real here. Share your struggles, share the pain that they have caused. Let people know that you are on the same level. This has a way of being extremely uncomfortable. It can even cause some trouble with the comfort zone dwellers in your church.

I have been very open about a lot of things in my past as I have started my ministry. I have decided that I never want people to think I am anything but a sinner saved by the grace of a loving God. As I have been writing this book, I have been sharing it with a friend, chapter by chapter. He has read it and given me some good insight into the book. He has a past just like everyone else. One day a man, who has obviously forgotten he, too, is a sinner saved by grace, was giving my friend a hard time about his past. My friend asked if the man had read any of my book and the man made the comment that he cannot believe that the church let me be a minister after all I have done. Did that hurt? I can't lie, it did. But you see this person was missing a few key points. First of all, nobody let me be a minister, God called me to be a minister. I don't know why. I am no more deserving of this calling than anyone else. Like Paul, when I look back on the way I have lived my life I consider myself to be the least of sinners and yet God has called me.

The second point is if God only called perfect people to the ministry, we only had one and we killed Him. The last point my brother in Christ missed was that all Christians are called to be ministers. Not necessarily to the pulpit, but to be ministers to share the Gospel, to be servants, etc. Being truthful about what Jesus has done in your life is not always easy but it is always the right thing to do.

You see the world doesn't need any more phonies, the world is full of them. They need people that are real. They need people who are not afraid to say, "look I am a sinner, just like you. I have fallen. I have stumbled. I have hurt people and I have been hurt. I am nothing great, but I have found an answer. Let me tell you about it..." We need to love people where they are because that's where Jesus met us. We need to stop trying to make people change. While we were yet sinners Jesus died for us. Think about the changes that Jesus made in your life. He will make the changes that He feels need to be made in their lives and from Him they will appreciate it. From us it would just be resented. The reason for that is it is not our job, it's His.

If you allow yourself to get comfortable eventually, I believe, you will become self-righteous. If you never come out of the prayer closet, I believe you will begin to forget about the havoc the enemy is wreaking on the world. You will sit in your little cocoon, watch the news, lament the condition of the world, and say, this world needs to know Jesus and then lock your door and go to sleep. If that is you, you are right, the world does need to know Jesus. If you don't tell them who will? You see, evil reigns when the church sits on its hands. When we do nothing but complain we become irrelevant. The last thing that this world needs is another group of people waving signs. Jesus didn't sit around waving a sign. Jesus didn't picket the temple with a sign that said, "Temple prices are not fair, Sacrifices are not wares." He got up, went in and turned over the tables.

As a person that has lived through two miscarriages, I am extremely pro-life. That being said, as of late I am beginning to question the methods of the pro-life community. I am less convinced than ever that carrying a sign and protesting a clinic is the way to go. You see I believe the answer to the abortion problem is the same as the answer to most, if not all, of the world's problems--Jesus Christ. Carrying a sign just gives the media something to talk about. It may serve some purpose somewhere down the line, but I would be happier to see the church making a very real effort to go into the community to reach young people with the Gospel of Jesus Christ. A Gospel that tells people to wait until marriage, a Gospel that tells the value Jesus places on children and on life, a Gospel that tells people a better way. You see I believe that God's Holy Spirit guiding people will make a difference in this world. Some mistakes will be made, sin will still occur, but the Gospel never comes back void.

The same could be said for prayer in school. The church has been lamenting this since 1963 (the year I was born) but what have we done about it? You see lamenting does very little. We need to be equipping our young people to come out of the prayer closet in our public schools. We need to help them to get to the point where they can and will lead on campus Bible studies, where they will lead a "See You at the Pole" group and most importantly where they will be unashamedly, Radically Real with their friends and classmates in the public schools. It will make the difference. The Gospel of Jesus Christ never comes back void. Hearts changed by Jesus become hearts that make a difference. People following the Word of God are people that live to make a difference. We need Radically Real kids in our schools that are willing to stand against the tide and show a faith that is real and relevant. We can help them. We can equip them. We can challenge them. We can pray for them. Not only can we, we must.

Is your church out of the prayer closet? Are you in your community making a difference? If the answer is yes, well done, keep moving forward. If the answer is no, Radically Real Christian the time is now to get busy. You may need to ruffle a few feathers; some feathers ruffle easily as the chickens are asked to leave the roost. But if the church is not out there in the world making a difference in the name of Jesus, is it really a church at all? You see the church is the body of Christ and it is high time we become his hands and feet and take his Gospel to a hurting world. In Him we can do it. All we need to do is leave our comfort zone.

Radically Real People from the Bible

Peter

Now I know what you are thinking, how on earth could the brash and bold, Peter be used as an example of being Radically Real and coming out of the prayer closet? After all, it was Peter who stepped out onto the water. It was Peter that cut off the ear of the man at Jesus arrest. This was not a man who was in the closet. But consider Peter in the Courtyard, consider Him denying Jesus three times before the rooster crowed. All of the sudden bold, brash Peter was in the closet. Now before we get too hard on Peter, I would like to remind you of something--Peter with a price on his head, more or less, was in the courtyard.

When that rooster crowed, Peter wept bitterly. This was Peter hitting bottom. He had let Jesus down. He said He would die with Jesus and here he was in the closet, denying Jesus. But something happened and here is what I think it is. Peter came out of the closet, slammed the door locked it and never went back. Peter left that day with a resolve. Peter was a new man. Peter was a man on a mission.

I have heard it said once that Peter and Judas had both let Jesus down, but only one of them came out of it. Judas denied Jesus and betrayed Him, but rather than make things right, Judas hung himself from a tree. Peter on the other hand repented of his betrayal. Too often we let our failures bury us and we find it safer never to leave the closet. We start our Christian walk all fired up but after a few rejections we lose heart, until eventually we figure that the world can fend for itself, we have found a comfort zone and we can just hide there and ride it out until we go Home. Peter knew that this was no way to live. Do You?

Peter headed the church in Rome during the time of great persecution. Peter urged the people to stay strong in their faith, even in the face of the persecution that they were facing at the hands of Nero. He told them the persecutions "...have come so that your faith--of greater worth than gold, which perishes even though refined by fire--may be proved genuine and may result in praise, glory and honor when Jesus Christ is revealed." Peter was a man refined. Peter became an evangelist. It was Peter in the second chapter of Acts that preached the Gospel and had over 3,000 conversions in one day. Keep in mind this is in the days before public address systems. Not bad for a guy that denied Jesus three times a short time ago. Peter was obedient until death even death on a cross.

Legend has it that Peter was crucified upside down because he didn't feel worthy to die the same way that Jesus died. Whether or not, one thing is true, the man that denied Jesus followed Him to the cross. And the next minute after He once again stood face to face with His old friend, who told Him, "Well done Peter, well done!" You can take that to the bank. How about you, where are you today? Are you in the closet? Are you sneaking around? Don't. The God that was with Peter is with you today. The God that took Peter from the fisherman to the leader of the church has an amazing plan for you, too. The God that picked someone who denied Him three times to lead His church is ready to forgive you. What are you waiting for? It's time to come out of the closet. It's time to leave the comfort zone and try God's plan on for size. C'mon you know you want to.

Chapter 12

What Part of Go Don't You Understand?

Radically Real Evangelism

Then the eleven disciples went to Galilee, to the mountains where Jesus had told them to go. When they saw Him, they worshipped him; but some doubted. Then Jesus came to them and said, "All authority in heaven and on earth has been given to me. Therefore **GO** *and make disciples of all nations, baptizing them in the name of the Father and of the Son and of the Holy Spirit, and teaching them to obey everything I had commanded you. And surely I am with you always, to the very end of the age."*

--Matthew 18:18-20

Imagine you are at the end of your life. What would you say to the ones that you love? What instructions would you give? What loose ends would you try to tie up? Last words are important. They are our last chance to influence the world before we leave it. Jesus' last words to us have long been called the Great Commission. Now I know at this point the letters will start flying so let me make this statement right here, right now. I do believe the Lord still speaks to us through His Holy Spirit, living in the hearts of all believers. And yet this moment on the mountain, before the ascension, is critically important. You see Jesus is leaving the physical world. From this point on, any believer will be one of those blessed believers that have not seen, as He described to Doubting Thomas. So His last words as a physical man, as the risen but still very physical Lord, are crucial. They are the instructions to both the ones He walked with and the generations to follow.

You see while we have not seen, we do not have a blind faith. We have a book written by the hand of God through witnesses who have seen these events (for the most part) first hand. We can trust the Word of God and we can trust its author even more. So, what are His instructions? Believers are to go into the world, all the world, not just the comfy parts and share His Good News with everyone that He places in our lives. It is absolutely essential that Radically Real Believers follow through on this commandment. The only way to salvation is Jesus Christ, period. If we as believers are unwilling to share, how can we expect anyone to take the Gospel seriously?

You see we are the ones that God has entrusted with His message. That's what Jesus was doing on that mountain. He was telling us to go out and spread the message, to reach the world. Those early Christians had a grip on the importance of that. They were willing to face lions and gladiators and persecution and martyrdom for the sake of the Gospel. And they did-- they reached far and wide for the Gospel. They (with the Holy Spirit) established the church and spread it. They gave their all to follow Jesus' Command. They were not perfect to be sure, but they were Radically Real.

Where are we today? Do we still have that missionary zeal? Do we still care about reaching our friends and neighbors with the Gospel? Before we say yes, I think we better think about where the church is today. The mainline churches are losing members in record numbers, there is still a large portion of the world that has not heard the Gospel. In America, it seems as though the society is moving further and further away from God. How can this be happening in a land that still has more religious freedom than many places in the world?

Don't even bother telling me about separation of church and state. Those words do not appear in the constitution. What does appear though is that, "Congress shall make no laws prohibiting the free practice of religion." The advances our society has made against Christianity have not been made on their own merits, they have been made by our complacency. You see what the constitution is really saying, is that we are not going to make a state religion, one that causes worship by force, which is not true worship. This is a great law designed to give us religious freedom. It has been corrupted against Christianity because the father of lies will always oppose the truth of the Gospel and too many of the children of God have sat silently and allowed him to have his way. In truth today in a lot of the western church, the Great Commission has become the Great Omission. We have left it out in favor of comfort and security. Look at the rest of the world. In places in the world where there is great persecution, like China, the church is growing in unprecedented numbers. People are convinced that they have found the truth that will set them free and they are willing to face imprisonment and even death to share it with the lost. It might cause one to ask the question, "Has the church is the west grown too comfortable?"

The state the Western church is in today is not irreparable. Greater is He that is in us that he that is in the world. It is time for the Western Church to make a stand for the truth.

Could it be that the church has forgotten? Could it be that we have stopped being the body of Christ and become a loose confederacy of social justice clubs? Could it be that we are no longer one body but rather a group of people that get together out of sense of obligation and tradition rather than out of a commitment to the risen Lord? Sadly. I believe, in too many cases the answer is yes. We are comfortable, we are happy and we have somehow come to the conclusion that we are more worthy of salvation than those outside the church because we observe the ritual of Sunday church attendance. Like the church in Laodicea, we have become lukewarm. The church that God said He would spew out. I don't know about you, but I would hate to stand before the throne of my God, having been part of the church that made God want to puke. If your church is not like the one I describe here, good for you, praise the Lord for His blessing and then ask Him to show you a church that your congregation can light a fire under for Him. You see in this day and age in America, it's not just the world, that is to say the lost, that needs evangelism. No, I believe that there need to be people that go to the church and call it back to its call to go into the world and making disciples of all nations.

Don't wait for someone else to take up the charge. Don't wait for others to do this for you, God has called you, me and every believer to share the Good News. I believe that if God had one message for the church in America and around the world, it would be, "What part of "GO" don't you understand?"

The Great Commission, What Is It?

Let's look at the Great Commission. The Lord has been crucified, and He has risen. He has spent the last forty days on the earth, showing himself to many and encouraging His followers. Now it is time for Him to return to the Father. To reassume the place He has held since before time began. His disciples are with Him there on the mountain top. The eleven that He has been training all along to lead the church and He wants to give them His final instructions. From now on He will guide them in a still small voice. So, this message for them is very important, and He speaks very clearly and concisely. Here is His message for them then and for us today.

"All authority on heaven and on earth has been given to me." Jesus is reminding them that He is not just Jesus the guy that they used to hang with, but rather that He is God and is returning to the Father. It is even more than that, however. It is Him saying, "Look, you are going to need me and I am still here. When you need help come to me. I have the power to help you. Everything in heaven and on earth is ultimately in my control." These guys have no reason to fear. They have walked with the Son of God and are on their way to fulfilling His mission. It is the same for us today. We have no reason to fear. We walk with Jesus and when we are reaching out into the world, we are fulfilling His mission for our lives. We are ultimately following the one who is in charge. As long as we are careful to seek His will, victory will be ours.

"Therefore go and make disciples of all nations," Boy, Jesus can say a lot in a few words. The basic premise is to "go." We are to leave our comfort zone and share His message. Where should we go? Well to all nations, in other words everywhere. It might be around the block, it may be around the world. It seems as though, if we are faithful in the small things, He will give us greater things to do. Not everyone will go on an overseas mission, but everyone has a mission field. Maybe it's your office, maybe it's your classroom

and maybe it's an underdeveloped part of Africa. Only God knows for sure, but the first step is always the same, to share our faith, we first have to go.

One more word on the phrase, "all nations." It should be clear from this phrase that there is no room for racism or prejudice in the kingdom of God. Those two words tell us God is open to everyone, that God loves the people of every nation. For too long people have taken His word out of context to support racism. This simple two-word phrase lets us know that it's His will that no one of any race or nation should perish. It also tells us that we are to reach out to all religions with the truth of the Gospel. No matter how politically incorrect it may sound, there is only one way into heaven, Jesus Christ and we are very clearly instructed to take this truth to everyone. It is inexcusable to think that we will only reach out to the unbeliever and let all the others sort out their faith with their own God. There is only one God. Jesus Christ is for everyone. There is no other way. Some will say that I am endorsing proselytizing. Let me be very clear on this point. I am! You see, if there is only one way to Heaven, then only one group is getting in. The ones who take Christ as Lord and Savior. This is not hateful, it is loving. I am not saying to reinstate the inquisitions here I am talking about love. Jesus said that He came into the world not to condemn it but to save it. We do not share Jesus as a way of condemnation, but so that everyone would have the chance to make the decision that will save their lives for all eternity. The most loving thing a person can do is to share their faith in Jesus.

Now after we go, what are we supposed to do? We are to make disciples. It is important that we look at this. This is not hit and run evangelism. This is not just to slap a tract in someone's hand as you run away. This is about becoming deeply involved in people's lives. This is about helping them to be followers of Jesus. It is about helping them to find a Bible-believing church home where they can grow in their faith and ultimately replicate themselves by going and making other disciples. It is a spiritual training process guided by the Holy Spirit. Too often we do not follow up, we get the decision and then we let go. Evangelism is more than just getting decisions. The decision is right, the decision is great, but the decision is just the first step. Decision without discipleship may be enough to get the person in the gate, but it is definitely not all that God intended for the person. The church has got to get past the notion that eternal life starts at the grave. Eternal life starts the day we ask Jesus Christ into our hearts to be our Lord and Savior. Jesus said that He came that we may have life and have it abundantly. That abundant life happens when people spend their lives following Jesus and seeing His plan unfold in their lives. That takes discipling.

Baptizing them in the name of the Father, and of the Son and of the Holy Spirit." Baptism is the outward sign of what God does in our lives when we accept Christ. It seems simple, doesn't it? And yet there are many different thoughts on baptism. Some baptize infants, for the sake of the original sin. Some baptize a person upon confession of faith, ("repent and be baptized.") and still others believe more in the baptism of the Holy Spirit. Each of these beliefs has some merit, but here is what is clearly the most important thing. Every believer, every Christian, has to believe in Jesus, every believer has to believe He was (and is) the Son of God. Every believer must believe that Jesus died on the cross for his sins and that He rose again from the Grave. Every believer must accept Christ as Lord and Savior. That is what is most important. Disagreements will always erupt among people, it is inevitable, but the church, if it is really the body of Christ, must be united in Christ.

"and teaching them to obey everything I have commanded you." This goes back to the idea of discipling the new believer. How do we know everything that Jesus has commanded us? The answer of course is by reading the Word of God. You see, far too often I believe we put too much of the spiritual training aspect of our lives in the hands of our pastors and Sunday School Teachers. While Sunday School and church are extremely important in the life of every believer, it is also essential that we let the Word of God speak to us directly. We should be testing everything that we hear from the pulpit or the lectern,

or even this book against the Word of God. Then after we have some insight into the Word of God, we should share that with others. To be a Radically Real Christian, it means that we seek to follow Jesus' example not just on Sunday but every day of our lives. We need to be carefully following God's commands.

Just because we are saved by grace, for example, does not mean we should sin with impunity, knowing that God will forgive us. No, we need to strive in the power of the Holy Spirit to "be perfect as our Father in Heaven is Perfect." Even though perfection on this side of the grave may not be possible for us, it is time for us to demonstrate Jesus to a world that has never seen Him. We cannot do that if we are not following His example and doing all that He has commanded. This is a big part of what being Radically Real is all about.

A lot of the world regards the church as nothing but a bunch of hypocrites. Part of this is because they hold confessing Christians to a different standard. This may seem unfair until we consider that, I believe, they are really looking for someone to get it right. They are looking for someone to show them a life that "walks the talk." The world is looking for a way to fill the emptiness. They are seeking it in all the wrong places and then one day they come upon a Christian. A Christian that is modeling joy, a Christian that is struggling to live righteously and is experiencing the abundant life that Jesus promised those that would follow Him. Not necessarily a life filled with wealth (if you are looking for "name it and claim it," you came to the wrong place) but rather a life with a purpose, not just an existence. A life that lets us face challenges with hope and confidence of knowing that God is in control. That is what this person has been looking for all along. When the world sees us living that kind of life they will want to know more. They will see the authenticity of a believer struggling for righteousness rather that a hypocritical, "wanna-be" saint. They will want to know Jesus by seeing you. That's what it means to be Radically Real. Then all you have to do is tell them.

The basic premise of this book is, "if being a Christian was a crime, would there be enough evidence to convict you?" The world is looking for the truth. The closest we can come to the truth is when we strive to obey all that Jesus commanded and admit to those who are watching when we struggle and fail. To take off the whitewashed exterior and show them a life that is real. In doing this, we demonstrate the best we can be in Christ. Admitting our failures shows people a God who has amazing grace to forgive. They want to know Him. They want to live under that kind of grace. The enemy has painted a lot of nasty pictures of God. It is up to each of us to show the real picture of God that He has shown us in our lives. Are you obeying all that He has commanded you? If not, ask Him to help you. We are taught best by example. What kind of example are you demonstrating? The world is looking for Him. Will they see Him in you?

"And surely I am with you always, to the very end of the age." This is where the comfort comes from. Jesus is with us always. We do not struggle alone. He is right there with us. Is He there when we hurt? He is there always. Is He there when we struggle? He is with us always. Is He there when we sin? He is with us always. Is He with us when we fail? He is with us always. When will He leave us? Never, He is with us always. Get the picture? We cannot lose Him, even if we tried. That's how strong His love is. Oh, we can ignore Him. He has given us free will. We can try to fight the devil and leave Him out of it. But when we are beaten and bloody and remember that we are in way over our heads all we have to do is call. He hasn't left. He is with us always.

If I were to give any advice to the young Christian, it would be this, "Pray without ceasing." Take Him into every battle. Free will was given to us so that we might choose to follow Him, rather than make us robots or puppets. We can choose to leave Him, but He never leaves us.

The other side of it is this, "If Jesus is with you always, where are you taking Him?" Are you taking him any place that He'd rather not be? Are you taking Him to movies that He'd just as soon not see? You are taking Him along on your dates, if you're not married. Is He proud of you? You are taking Him to work or school. Is He pleased with your conduct there? You are taking Him home. Is He pleased with your priorities and does He feel welcome? These may seem like difficult questions but this is what you deal with, with an omnipresent God. Ask yourself this question, "What would the world be like if everyone lived as if Jesus was watching?" You see He is. He has promised to be with us always. He is there to fight your battles and He is there to share our joy. What an awesome God we serve, that He would want to be involved in every aspect of our lives. Let's make sure that every aspect of our lives gives glory and honor to Him.

A Command, Not A Request

You will notice one thing in looking at the Great Commission. Jesus says, "Therefore go." This is not a request. Jesus is not saying, "If you feel like it...," "If it's not too much trouble...," "When you have a free moment...," "When it's convenient..." He simply says, "GO." It is a command. He is telling us to go out and share our faith. It is every bit as much a command as "love your neighbor as yourself" or any of the others. Speaking of which maybe at this point we should ask the question:

"If You Don't Share Your Faith, Do You Really Love?"

I am always reminded of Jesus asking Peter, "do you love me?" Three times he asks the question. Every time Peter says, "Yes, Lord you know I do." Then Jesus says some variation of, "feed my sheep." Now if you are fairly new to the faith, you may not get this passage and in truth I didn't get it either until very recently. Jesus, of course, is not talking about sheep. He is talking about his "flock," the people. Not just his followers, though clearly

Jesus wanted Peter to lead them, but also the lost sheep, those outside faith in Him. Jesus is also not speaking only about physical food or physical needs but also about the spiritual food, the Good News, otherwise known as the Gospel. What Jesus is really saying to Peter is, "if you love me, tell people about me." I believe He is saying the same thing to us today. "Christian, if you love me, share me. Tell people about me. Tell them I love them. Tell them they can find hope in me. Tell them I am the way to Heaven and I want to see them there." This is not just some cry across 2000 years of history. This is the living God, the Holy Spirit tugging at our hearts to share the Good News of Salvation in Jesus Christ. If we love Him, we will share Him.

In John 14:6, Jesus says, "I am the way and the truth and the life, no one comes to the Father except through me." No one comes to the Father except through Jesus. No one goes to Heaven without Jesus. If people do not go to Heaven, where do we go? I am sorry, I do not believe in purgatory. So therefore, the choices are simple, Heaven or Hell. So we must again ask ourselves the question, "If we don't share our faith, do we really love?"

To me it is quite obvious that if we don't share Jesus with people, we are really saying we don't care whether or not they go to Hell. To say you love someone and then not tell them about Jesus is a lie. Jesus is the only way to Heaven. I'm sure by now I've said that enough that you know I am serious about it. We need to be telling people about Jesus every chance you get. You never know when you might be the last person ever to get to tell them. Don't wait. Don't think, "well, someone else will do it." Pray and proceed. When God gives you an opportunity to share Him, take it. Somewhere I hear a voice saying, "how will I know if it is an opportunity?" A couple of things come to mind:

A question is an opportunity. When a person asks you a question about your faith it is like an engraved invitation to share. Answer the question truthfully even if your answer is, "I don't know." Remember, Jesus said, "I am the truth." This is no time to make something up. We are striving to be

Radically Real here. Tell them you'll get back to them and then get back to them. You may even get a chance to say, something like, "I don't have all the answers yet, but I can tell you that I know that the Bible is true." This is a statement that will get even the most hard-hearted unbeliever to ask how you can know. Then tell them it's because of how He has made a difference in your life and them tell them your story. Pray for opportunities like this.

A good deed is an opportunity. Take time to help someone. Take the time to make a difference. Then when they thank you, give the glory to God (where it belongs). Tell them that you helped them because of the way Jesus helped you.

Meeting an old friend can be an opportunity. Not everyone has the kind of gory rescue story that I have but everyone has a story. As I meet some people from my past and I share with them that I am now in the ministry, I usually get a response that is somewhere, a somewhat uncomfortable "Oh" to "Get the (fill in your favorite expletive here [incidentally if you are striving to be Radically Real you should no longer have a favorite expletive]) out!!" I usually try to relate by talking about the old days. Then as I break the ice and let them know that I still care about them, that I am not judging them (not my job, remember) and I begin to tell them about what's been happening in my life since I met Jesus.

"Chance" meetings are opportunities. You strike up a conversation with someone. You overhear someone make a comment about a book you have read. You share a common interest with someone. A person sits next to you on the bus or plane. You sit next to another parent at a little league game. I put chance in quotes because I believe a God that can create a universe leaves nothing to chance. The times we meet up with people for no apparent reason may well be new opportunities God is giving. Remember though, people are not opportunities, people are children of God. It is vital that we treat them with respect and get to know them. This is not hit and run evangelism. I believe that evangelism must be to some degree relational. You may not have hours to develop a relationship, but get to know something about the person before you witness. Invite them to your church if you are close by. Share a story. Never be rude. Don't make judgments.

Someone insulting the church, Christians or God may be an opportunity. This seems like a weird one, and scary, but it is entirely possible that the person doesn't understand or they are hurting or they are wounded, maybe by a past involvement with a church. Talk to the person. See if you can get them to explain their feelings. Then share, honestly and joyfully about your experience with God. It is important that you take note of this next statement: God does not need you to defend Him. He is God. Do not get angry with the person. Remember to see them as God sees them. He would want to wrap His arms around this hurting sinner and save Him, just like He did for you. Love this person. Jesus died for Him. Hang in there with them, unless you feel God telling you to give up for now. (This is not to be confused with your own discouragement).

The previous were five opportunities. There are many more. The truth is, we never know when an opportunity will come up, so we must always be "prayed up" and ready. Pray that God will reveal opportunities to share Him with others. In this chapter we have looked at a lot of aspects of evangelism. There are a few more things to be said.

Usually when we think of evangelism, we tend to think of evangelists like Billy Graham and thousands of people hearing the Word. Dr. Graham is a hero of mine and I respect him immensely. If God is calling you to do that style of evangelism, praise him and go out and do it. But this is not the only way to do evangelism. Most of us are simply called to go out to our friends and neighbors one on one, one soul at a time. That is OK, as a matter of fact that is often how Jesus did it. The important thing in evangelism is never the numbers. If people become numbers to us we will probably never reach them. The important thing in evangelism is helping people to find Jesus. Some may go to Africa or China, some may go to the inner city and some may have to go no further than their own back yard. The important thing is not where you go. The important thing is that you follow God's call and go.

Radically Real Examples from the Bible

The Demoniac

Now I know what you're thinking. "Poor guy got almost all the way through his first book only to lose his mind. He somehow thinks that the story of a guy that ran around naked among the tombs, will tell us something we need to know about evangelism." Trust me, I haven't lost it. Check it out. Here we have a guy that was out of his mind. We don't even know his name but some translations call him the Demoniac.

Near the Sea of Galilee, there was an area where tombs were carved out of stone cliffs. This is the domain of the Demoniac. He was so dangerous that he was bound in chains by his hands and feet with irons and heavy chains, but he was so strong that he broke them. He ran around naked, and cry out day and night and deliberately cut himself. To say this man was in pain and suffering would be to put it very mildly.

Jesus and the disciples landed their boat on the shore and this maniac ran out to meet them. I can almost imagine the disciples saying, "Master, maybe we should get out of here." Could you blame them? But Jesus has a different plan.

When they land, the man falls on his knees before them. The voice that comes from his mouth tells the tale. It is a voice so evil that it curls your hair. Demons! Notice the first thing the demons do is try to claim their rights. Then the voice begs, "What do you want with me, Jesus, son of the most high God? Swear to God that you won't torture me!" Jesus doesn't even flinch. He knows that the demons are powerless against Him.

Jesus says, "Come out of that man you evil spirit." Jesus asks his name, the demon doesn't have a real name, he's speaking for the crowd.

He says, "My name is Legion for WE are many." The demons must like the neighborhood, because they keep on asking Jesus not to make them leave the area.

Eventually Jesus casts them into a herd of pigs, and as soon as they enter the pigs, they drive them that crazy that the pigs run off the cliff and drown in the sea. Needless to say, the guys that owned the pigs freaked. It's not bad enough that they have to put up with the howling of this maniac that lives among the graves but now this other guy pulls up, says a few words and all their pigs run into the sea. What they see next, is even more amazing. The maniac is dressed and in his right mind. They were scared to death. So scared that they asked Jesus to leave the area. What a strange breed we are. We see the power of God and we ask Him to leave.

Meanwhile back on the beach, the demoniac is free for the first time in his life. It is time for Jesus to leave to go onto the next place but the man does not want Him to leave. You can imagine that this man must find his freedom almost incomprehensible. There is only one thing that he knows for sure, if Jesus is going, he is going with Him. He has been freed and he will follow Jesus anywhere.

By now you are thinking, nice story, Biblical even, but what does this have to do with evangelism. I am getting to that right now. Look what Jesus did next. Jesus sent him home. Jesus tells him to go home to his family, home to his old neighborhood and TELL THEM WHAT THE LORD HAS DONE FOR HIM. Do you realize what just happened here? Jesus has just commissioned His first evangelist. This man that had so many demons in him that they drove a whole herd of pigs into the sea is now to go and tell his story. (Can you imagine that testimony??) This man that no chains could hold is now a slave to Jesus, going to the ten towns around his home and sharing the good news. Then comes the greatest understatement in the whole Bible. When the demoniac told his story, "all the people were amazed."

My question for you, Radically Real Christian is this, if this man with all these demons, and all this pain, all this history and all this stuff going against him can go out and spread the Gospel--what's your excuse?

Chapter 13

If It Ain't Broke...

Radically Real Commitment

Now one of the Pharisees invited Jesus to have dinner with him, so He went to the Pharisee's house and reclined at the table. When a woman who had lived a sinful life in that town learned that Jesus was eating at the Pharisee's House, she brought an alabaster jar of perfume, and as she stood behind Him at His feet weeping, she began to wet his feet with her tears. Then she wiped them with her hair, kissed them and poured perfume on them.

When the Pharisee who had invited Him, saw this, he said to himself, "If this man were a prophet, He would know who is touching Him and what kind of woman she is-- that she is a sinner."

Jesus answered him, "Simon, I have something to tell you."

"Tell me teacher," he said.

"Two men owed money to a certain money lender. One man owed him five hundred denarii, and the other fifty. Neither of them had the money to pay him back, so he cancelled the debts of both. Now which of them will love him more?"

Simon replied, "I suppose the one who had the bigger debt cancelled."

"You have judged correctly," Jesus said.

Then he turned toward the woman and said to Simon, "Do you see this woman? I came into your house. You did not give me water for my feet, but she wet my feet with her tears and wiped them with her hair. You did not give me a kiss, but this woman, from the time I entered has not stopped kissing my feet. You did not put oil on my head, but she has poured perfume on my feet. Therefore I tell you her many sins have been forgiven--for she loved much. But he who has been forgiven little loves little."

Then Jesus said to her, "Your sins are forgiven."

--Luke 7: 36-50 (NIV)

There's an old saying, "If it ain't broke, don't fix it." That sounds like sound advice. You don't tear your car's engine apart if you're not having problems with it and yet in our own lives and in the church, sometimes we have a difficult time determining if something is broken. We often go along with the status quo, oblivious and comfortable but having a hard time moving forward. In the story of Jesus, the Pharisee and the sinful woman from Luke chapter 7, we see two people in a state of brokeness that come in contact with the master repairman, if you will, Jesus Christ.

These two people are a study in contrast, the holy man of God and the prostitute. One is a respected member of society; the other is basically an outcast and yet in the end the outcast is "in" and the holy man is "out." As we look at the story there are two main characters who are interacting with the third main character, Jesus. Over and over in the scriptures we are treated to seeing the wisdom of Jesus. Luke 7:36-50 shows us once again how incredibly wise Jesus was and is. This story shows a comparison of attitudes that is a great example for us today.

Let's start by looking at the woman. Some translations say that she was a prostitute, others say she was a sinful woman. Either way, her life was clearly not as it should be. She was struggling in a painful existence, with seemingly no way out. Yes, she was a sinner. Yes, many of her wounds were self-inflicted and yet here she was. You can imagine her looking for a way out of all this and yet feeling that the hole she had dug for herself was just too deep. She needed help. Help was on the way.

How many people do you know in this situation? People that seem to be wallowing in sin, struggling to climb out of the hole that they have dug for themselves with no hope in sight. The hole they have dug is so deep. Often it is combined with a directional problem. They look in the wrong direction and end up trying to dig their way out of the hole. They rely on their own strength rather than God strength and when they do that it always ends up in disaster. The problem is this, when you find yourself in a hole, the way out is up. Always up. We need to look up to the one that is reaching His loving hand out to help us. When we rely on our own strength, we try to dig our way out. Well, you can dig and dig and dig but two things will eventually happen. The hole you are in will just get deeper and deeper and eventually you will end up in a place where everything is really hot. You see if you get far enough down in the earth, it gets hotter and hotter until you get to the molten core of the earth. Similarly, in life if we get stuck in our own sin and we keep trying in our own power we just get deeper in. Eventually we end up in a hole we cannot leave.

Getting out of the hole is easy. All we have to do is reach our hands up. And here's where Radically Real Christians come in. You see God wants us to be on the lookout for people in holes. And God wants us shouting our message of hope into the holes and showing people the way out. God wants us to help people to stop digging and start climbing. Let's look at the story a little further.

One day the woman heard that Jesus was coming to town. She had probably heard about all the great things that Jesus was doing and thought, "maybe this great teacher can help me." You see don't miss this, she has stopped digging and is starting to look the other way. Take a minute and think about the courage this woman had. Her examples of religious leaders were not like many of the fine pastors we have today. Her examples were the Pharisees. They were proud men who were very judgmental and very much sold-out to legalism.

The church has to be careful not to fall into that trap. When we forget that we are to be lighthouses in a dark world and instead look at our own righteousness we fail in our mission to reach the world and we leave people like this woman to try to dig their way out. The woman had no way of knowing that Jesus was going to accept her but she had to try. The Pharisees would have taken one look at her and sent her away. You could say she was desperate, but Radically Real Christians will look at this woman and see that she had immense courage. Look at your congregation? Are you more like Jesus or more like the Pharisees? How would they (or for that matter you?) react if they saw this woman. It is clear from our story How Jesus would react. Let's continue on in our story.

Notice that when the woman comes, she does not come empty handed. She brings something of great value to offer Jesus, an alabaster jar of perfume. Later in Jesus' ministry, a similar event to this happens. A woman comes to Jesus with a similar bottle of perfume. We find from that passage, that a bottle such as this would be worth a year's wages. The woman came with the intent of giving what she has to offer. It may pale in comparison to what Jesus has to offer, but it is what she has and possibly all she has. Do we do that? Do we offer all we have to Jesus or do we treat him like some celestial Santa Claus and just take, take, take? The blessings of God are given to us so that we may use them to serve His Kingdom. Radically Real Christians seek daily to do the will of God and to use their blessings to serve Him. What we have pales in comparison to what to the gift of eternal life, but Radically Real Christians realize that all we have belongs to God and we are most blessed when we use His gifts to serve His Kingdom.

Let's go back to the story. I think we have to take a minute and look at the scene here. We have a little bit of a distorted view of what this scene may have looked like. Pieces of art like DaVinci's "Last Supper" show Jesus and his disciples sitting at a long table eating. It looks almost as if Jesus told the disciples to move to one side of the table so that everyone could get in the picture. It's not likely, given the culture of the time, that the scene looked that way. No, more likely the guests at the dinner would have sat around the room on couches to eat. They would have reclined on these couches, feet outstretched with their heads near the table propping themselves up on one elbow. From now on you will have to use your imagination. Put yourself on one of those couches and watch the King of Kings in action.

You are comfortably eating a meal in the home of Simon the Pharisee. Simon is a very important man and you feel honored to be there. Today is an extra special occasion because today is the day that that new teacher that has everyone in an uproar is here. They say that He has been doing all kinds of miracles all over the place, perhaps you'll get to see one today. You hear a murmur start to rise up in the room and you turn to see this woman enter the room. You would think she was quite beautiful if you didn't know what she did for a living. And look at how she is dressed, why she isn't even trying to hide what kind of a woman she is. She is sobbing uncontrollably and she is carrying an alabaster jar of expensive perfume. She walks through the room and sits herself down quietly at the feet of Jesus. "Whoa," you think, "maybe the Pharisees are right about this guy after all." As you look at the scene unfolding, some thoughts arise in your mind, questions if you will. You think, "Who is she?"; "Why is she here?"; "Why is she trying?" You might even be thinking, "What nerve she has to come barging in here, clearly she was not invited!" Then you have a recollection, "Oh I know who she is, I have seen her working the street corner downtown."; "How dare she get near the Teacher like that."; "Why doesn't He send her packing?"; "Oh great, now look what she's done, with all her sobbing and carrying on she has made His feet all wet."; "Now look she's drying his feet with her hair. How disgusting!"; "I can't believe He's putting up with this."; "He must just be too embarrassed to say anything."; "Oh and now look at this, kissing His feet."; "Oh no! What is she doing now?"; "Doesn't she know how expensive that perfume is?"; "She is pouring it on His feet."; "Why doesn't He stop her?"; "She is making a scene!"

Yes, she was making a scene but it is really much more important than that. You see, I believe that when she came into the presence of Jesus, she saw herself in His light and realized how unworthy she was to be in His presence. In that moment she came face to face with her own sin. You see when we look at the perfection of Jesus, we cannot help but realize how very sinful and unworthy we are. I believe that is the reason so many people in that day hated Jesus. They were so set in their ways that when Jesus in His perfection came along, rather than seeing His love and His forgiveness they became caught up in their own imperfections. Their pride kept them from seeing the light, and so they returned to the darkness of their hearts. Things haven't changed that much in the last 2,000 years. And while it is true, that even at our best we are pale reflections of Jesus when we let our lights shine some will run to it and others will run to the darkness and maybe even plot against us. That is what we are up against as Radically Real Christians. But the good news is this, the one who has had victory over sin and the grave, is on our side. We need not battle alone. When we fall to our knees and trust in the Lord, He will be faithful and help us. He will even draw some of those who plot against us into the light if we remain Radically Real.

It was this conviction that the woman was under right now. She saw her own sin but rather than run and hide she wanted to walk away changed. She wanted to be forgiven. Let's look at what she did. Did she look Him in the eye and say, "well if you think I'm bad you should see Bertha, she is much worse than me?" No, she couldn't even look Him in the eye. She fell at his feet. She humbled herself and served Him. His feet were dirty. She would wash them. She took what she had and used it. She washed His feet with her tears and dried them with her hair. Take a minute and really think about that act. There are few acts in the whole Bible that are more humble. This woman is under deep conviction. Imagine crying enough that you could use those tears to wipe the grime of a day of walking dirt streets in sandals away. This woman desires to make a change in her life and she knows that at this very moment she is face to face with the only one that can help her.

This is the same kind of humility that Radically Real Christians need to exhibit every day of our lives. If you are Radically Real, you cannot afford to ever think that you are too good. Only through Jesus do we have any goodness at all. It is that attitude that we need when we approach the lost. Then she did another thing that we must consider, she took her expensive perfume and poured it on His feet. Remember that we already established that this perfume could have been worth as much as a year's wages. Don't miss this. She took what she had of value, what the world considers valuable and poured it at the feet of the Master. Radically Real Christians must do the same thing. We must take the things of this world and lay them at the foot of the cross if we are to succeed at fulfilling our mission. Remember earlier in this book we looked at the blessings of God and determined that everything we have is blessing from God and it is to be used to His Glory to fulfill His mission for your life.

Notice what Jesus does. He tells the woman her sins are forgiven. Can't you picture Him, with compassion overflowing, knowing her sin and feeling her pain? Can't you just see Jesus, reaching out His hand, helping her to her feet, looking her in the eye and saying, "Your faith has saved you, go in peace." Now she was forgiven. Now she had peace, now she had a chance to start over. This woman saw the brokenness in her life and knew where to go to be repaired. She fell at Jesus' feet broken; He lifted her up whole. She deserved judgment. She received grace. Radically Real Christians must model that same attitude. We cannot afford to feel any sense of superiority. Christians are not better than anyone else. What we are is better off. In Jesus we have forgiveness, we have peace and we have a reason to try to do all things better to bring glory to God. We have hope in a hopeless world. All these things are blessings from God, gifts we do not deserve, gifts that must be shared with the hurting people of the world. That is what it means to be Radically Real.

Challenging the Church

Now we come to Simon the Pharisee. But before we begin, I would like to make a statement. You see I believe that as we look at the scriptures that whenever Jesus speaks to the Pharisees, that should be seen as an "attitude check" for the church. Jesus' conversation with Simon the Pharisee is certainly no exception. Let's look at it closer.

Simon had invited Jesus into his home. We're not sure why exactly. Perhaps he was curious about Jesus. Perhaps he was trying to learn from Jesus. Perhaps he was trying to see what all the fuss was about or perhaps he specifically wanted to trap Jesus in something he could incriminate Him with. We can't tell for sure but he extended the invitation and Jesus came.

You know we always look at the Pharisees as the enemy, the "Biblical bad guys" and yet all the sects of Judaism at the time, the Pharisees were the closest in their beliefs to Jesus. The Saducees rejected the resurrection of the dead. The Zealots were looking to solve their problems and take power by whatever means necessary, including violence. By comparison, the Pharisees believed in resurrection and eternal life and were largely a peaceful bunch because they were too law-abiding to be violent. The only acts of violence they would have permitted were those allowed in Levitical law. If we were to have some Pharisees around here in this day and age, I believe we would find them to be godly people. They kept the law; they spent a lot of time in the scriptures and in prayer. In short, if we were to look at the Pharisees today, we would probably say that they are good people. And yet as close as they were in their beliefs, it was the Pharisees that sought to kill Jesus. In fairness, it is important to remember one thing however. The Pharisees didn't kill Jesus, although they did plot and bring the charges. Neither did the Romans kill Jesus, although they did wash their hands of Him and they drove the nails. No, Jesus was killed (in the flesh), by you and I and our sin. Radically Real Christians always remember that.

Why did the Pharisees dislike Jesus so much? Let's look at Simon for some clues. To start off with, when the woman touches Jesus, Simon automatically jumps into "judgment mode". He judges the woman and he judges Jesus. He thinks, "Surely Jesus can't be a prophet, because if He was, He would know what kind of woman is touching Him." For the record, Jesus knew exactly who was touching Him, and all that she had done and everything else, but Jesus was filled with love and compassion and He knew He could help. That is the attitude Radically Real Christians need to have when dealing with the lost!

Incidentally, Jesus also knew exactly what Simon was thinking. We need to avoid getting into "judgment mode." Simon became judgmental. Do we do that? Now before you jump and say "no" picture another scene in your mind. You are sitting in your comfortable pew in church, third row from the front. One day, you are sitting there doing your best to give the proceedings your full attention when you begin to hear a murmur from the back of the church. Finally, you can contain your curiosity no longer and you turn around to see a woman walking down the aisle. She is wearing a pink wig, a leather jacket over a metallic gold top. She finishes the ensemble with a zebra print miniskirt, knee high, high heel boots and fish net stockings. She goes to the seat in front of you falls to her knees in prayer sobbing her eyes out. What would you do? Would you be giving God a spiritual "high-five," and saying, "Yes God!! One of [you] wayward children is coming home." Or would you nudge your neighbor and say "uh-oh, there goes the neighborhood. What is she doing here?" I think it is pretty clear from our story what Jesus' reaction would be. Let's check our attitude and act accordingly.

Jesus then goes into what I have found to be His most powerful teaching tool, the parable. A parable is a simple story used to illustrate a point. This is, in my humble opinion, one of His best. He speaks of a man who has lent two men sums of money. One he loaned a fairly small amount, say $50. To the other he loaned a larger amount, for example $50,000. Both of these guys fell on hard times. The bills are piling up, they are shutting off the electricity, the car's been repossessed, you name it. Bottom line, neither of these guys can pay up. The man who loaned the money is very rich and so he decides, out of the kindness of His heart to forgive both of the debts. Which one would have loved him more? Easy question, right? One guy owes him an expensive dinner, the other owes him a cheap house. The one who owes him the most also, it would stand to reason would love him the most.

And so it goes with God. We are all indebted to God. Some people's debts may appear to be greater than others and yet the Bible tells us that all have sinned and fallen short of the glory of God. Simon sees only the woman as the sinner, he feels justified in himself. No Radically Real Christian can ever afford to feel that way. We are all sinners and we cannot ever afford to forget that salvation was a free gift that we neither deserved nor earned. In this story, it is easy for the woman to see her sin and her need for salvation. She is humble and repentant and she walks away from this encounter with Jesus, whole and forgiven. Simon on the other hand is proud of himself and his own righteousness and cannot see his need for salvation. But never fear. Simon is about to receive a nice big slice of humble pie.

Simon agrees with Jesus. The one that owed much would love much. Then Jesus, in His own truly amazing way brings the story home. He says to Simon, "Do you see this woman?" "I came into your house and you didn't give me any water for my feet." This was a common courtesy, folks. These people walked dirt streets in sandals all day long. Their feet got filthy. When you entered someone's home, they would give you water to wash up with. Simon was an important person in this culture and yet he ignored this common courtesy. Simon was falling down on the job. Jesus continues, "but this woman wet my feet with her tears and wiped them with her hair. "You did not give me a kiss..." This was common greeting in that culture. It was a show of respect. It seems as if Simon was showing Jesus an extreme lack of respect. Maybe Simon thought he was too good to serve Jesus in this way. Radically Real Christians take note, the way you treat all people is important. We always need to be gracious, well-mannered and kind if we want to follow the example set before us in Christ. This does not mean weakness, but rather that we realize that the people that come into our lives, no matter what place they are in are also children of God. It does not mean we "sugar-coat" the truth, but it does mean that we speak the truth in love.

Jesus continues, "but from the time I entered this woman has not stopped kissing my feet." There is a question about what Simon actually thinks of Jesus. It appears that he may not have been showing Jesus the respect He deserves. On the other hand, there is absolutely no question what the woman thinks of Jesus. She knows that she is unfit to be in the same room with him. She knows her role. We also have to remember that. You see the fact that Jesus has made himself accessible to us does not negate the fact that He is God! "You did not put oil on my head, but she has put perfume on my feet." Again, Simon neglected the common courtesy, but the woman in her humility went above and beyond the call of duty. Then Jesus drives it home! "Therefore, I tell you, her many sins are forgiven -- for she loved much. But he who has been forgiven little, loves little." Ouch!! Can't you see Simon cringe? Again, in this we see a challenge for the church and for Radically Real Christians everywhere. Maybe you have lived your whole life in the church. Maybe you have lived a pretty clean and upright life. But the bottom line is we are all sinners who have fallen short of the glory of God. When we deal with the people that God has put in our life, we always need to remember that it is by the grace of God that we are saved and not by our works or righteousness or anything else. Because we know that all have sinned, we also know that one sin in your whole life is enough to disqualify you from Heaven.

The problem is that we look at sin in degrees. We see one sin as being worse than another sin and God doesn't. To Him sin is sin. I might look at someone and say, "Well I may not be perfect but I'm better than Bob." The problem is that Bob is not my standard. The person you compare yourself to, to make yourself feel better is not your standard. The Man who took the cross for you is your standard. Jesus Christ, the perfect Lamb of God is your standard. The standard is perfection and we are all short of it. Radically Real Christians need to be humble. We need to remind ourselves that we are nothing without Jesus. It is His grace we need to make us whole!

The sinful woman looked at herself in the mirror of Jesus and saw that she needed to make a change. She humbled herself before the Lord and the Lord lifted her up and gave her peace and forgiveness and a new start. Simon the Pharisee had a problem. He was using the wrong mirror. He used the mirror of the folks around him and got a distorted image of himself. He was broken too he just couldn't see it. Are we doing this in the church today? Are we looking at others and finding ourselves better or are we looking at ourselves in the perfect mirror of Jesus Christ and finding where we come up lacking? And then, do we give our lives to the master repairman and allow Him to make us whole?

Friends, there is a problem in the church today. It is widespread across the whole body of Christ. We have spent so much time comparing ourselves to one another and to the outside world, that we have become comfortable in our own filthy rags of righteousness. It is a lot less painful, in the short run, to go along as we are, fat and happy in our own distorted image. The problem with that is simple. We are not made in our own image; we are made in God's image. The church is His church and our comfort is not His primary concern. The lost are His primary concern. Jesus, our example, did not die in His sleep in a lazy boy. Jesus went to a hard wooden cross with nails in His hands and feet for the lost. We are told to go into the world with the good news. The church has got to leave its comfort zone. We have to be out there, out there where the folks think we're crazy, out there with the folks that think we're bigots and all those other things. Why? Because when it is all said and done, in Jesus, we are right. Why? Because from the Word of God we know how this story ends and we are on the winning team! Why? Because He said so!!

The church is walking around with the attitude of "if it ain't broke, don't fix it." What we should be saying is "if it ain't broke, BREAK IT!" Our unwillingness to leave our comfort zone is leaving people hanging off a cliff with the flames of Hell licking at their feet. It is time for a change. It is time for Radically Real Christians to make a stand. It is time for the body of Christ, the church, to find its fire again. The church needs to stop looking at the world's standard and start aiming at God's standard.

The church is slipping because we are looking in the wrong direction to solve our problems. We look to political solutions to so many problems when we should be looking to God. You see I believe we have what I call "heart problems".

The heart problems will never, ever be fixed by legislation. Violence will never be stopped by gun control, violence will stop (or at least slowed down) with hearts being changed by Jesus. Abortion will never be stopped by legislation. Abortion is a heart problem. How else can it be explained that a rational human being accept that it is OK to kill an innocent child? Abortion will only ever be stopped when people's hearts are changed by Jesus.

You name the issue that we face today, most of them are heart problems. We can make laws until we all have writer's cramp and we still will not have made a dent. The answer to any and all heart problems is the same, hearts being changed by Jesus. Church, when are we going to stop letting the government do our job? It is the church's job to reach out with the Gospel of Jesus Christ.

Make no mistake about it, Jesus Christ will make the difference. Radically Real Christians have got to stop carrying signs and start carrying the Gospel to a hurting word, otherwise we are treating the symptoms and ignoring the underlying disease. When the disease is cured the symptoms will go away, and not the other way around. Am I saying that Christians have no business in politics? Absolutely not! You should vote. But when you vote, you should have the newspaper in your left hand and the word of God in your right. You should pick the candidate from the left hand that matches up best with what you have in your right hand. If God leads you to run for office, run. Just remember a Christian doesn't stand on polls and focus groups, a Christian stands on the Word of God.

The church needs to wake up!! It's not a sleep of faith, it's a leap of faith. Many people complain about the welfare system. Before welfare, who took care of the poor? It was the church serving in the name of Jesus Christ. And let me tell you, we did a better job. Why? Because God was with us. People were being fed and souls were being won for the Kingdom. The system today is marred with inefficiency and worse. Twenty-eight cents of every welfare dollar actually goes to helping someone. The laws concerning distribution of benefits encourage illegitimacy and discourage marriage and strong families. See what happens when we let the government do the work of the body of Christ.

The church (not the whole church, but enough of it that I think this is a fair statement to make) comforts itself in the fact that government is taking care of the poor. Some people are even considering their taxes as part of their tithe, even though Jesus very clearly said "render unto Caesar what is to Caesar's and unto the Lord what is the Lord's." In the next breath, we look around and lament the state the world is in. Radically Real Christians see a problem, pray for guidance and then get to work.

So, who are you today? Are you like the sinful woman who saw herself in the light of Jesus, humbled herself and was given peace, forgiveness and a new start? Or are you like Simon the Pharisee, looking at others as your standard, failing to see your own brokenness and satisfied with the status quo. Keep in mind one thing about the Pharisees. They may have been good people in the eyes of the world but they became so caught up in their own "filthy rags righteousness" that they missed the Messiah they had been praying for, for centuries, when He stood right before their eyes. My prayer is that Radically Real Christians would always want to be made whole.

Many Parts One Body

Throughout this book I have referred to the church as the body of Christ. I, of course, did not invent this phrase, it is written all over the Bible. But it really says a great deal about the role of Christians in our society. We are to be acting as the hands and feet of Jesus Christ serving his kingdom in His name. Some of us are to be His eyes, seeing what he wants us to see. Seeing the needs in our world and directing the body to the way to best serve. All the while realizing that with God as the Brains of the operation, we are doing His will and serving in His name. Some of us are to be the mouth, speaking and communicating the words we get from the "Brain". Some of us are the hands reaching out to the world with the love of Christ who lives in the heart of the body. And lastly some of us are the feet that go out and serve as directed by the heart and the brain.

Now this may be a bit oversimplified. Some of us that are called to speak will also serve and some that are called to serve will also speak and so on, but the fact of the matter remains that each person is given gifts to do something and be a part of the body. And all the parts of the body are vitally important. The "mouths" are no more important than the "feet." Each of us is called to use the gifts we have been given to serve the Kingdom. If the parts of the body are listless and lazy the body becomes weak. Everyone must be doing his or her part.

Do Something! Lead, Follow or Get Out of the Way!

Everyone who calls upon the name of the Lord has a job to do. Now I want to make a statement here so that I am not misunderstood. You cannot earn salvation, period. Salvation is a gift from God. It is by God's grace that we are saved and none of us are worthy. And yet out of appreciation for the great gift God has given, every Radically Real Christian should seek to do his part. The Word says "faith without works is dead". Is that strong enough for you? Salvation is not the end of the journey. It is the beginning. Why do you think they call it "born again"?

So, what should you do? For everyone the answer is the same, to live a life that glorifies God, serve others in the Name of Jesus and spread the Gospel (tell people about Jesus). That is pretty much our mission. It is when we get to "how" that the variety comes in. God gives us all these talents and spiritual gifts to serve His Kingdom. No two people are gifted exactly alike but each of us is called to use those gifts we have been blessed with. Much like the parable of the talents, one day Jesus is going to ask us all what we have done with what He is given us. What will you tell Him?

Lead

Some people are called to lead. They have a gift for it. You can tell it. They are the type of person that can keep a cool head under pressure. Jesus tells us in the Parable of the Talents that those who are faithful in the small things will be given more. Those that are called to lead always seem to be rising to the occasion. Make no mistake about it, however, if God is calling you to lead you will know. Trust Him to be faithful. You may not consider yourself to be a leader, but if God calls you, He will also equip you. You just have to be faithful. I remember hearing Rebecca St. James say something that has stuck with me ever since. She said, "God doesn't call the qualified, He qualifies the called". No truer words were ever spoken.

Consider Moses. Moses had a speech impediment. He was in hiding after having murdered a slave driver in Egypt, and God called Him to go into Egypt to lead His people to freedom and the promised land. Did Moses feel qualified for this mission? Absolutely not, but God called Him and God was faithful in equipping Moses with everything He needed. Moses was faithful when God called and led the people with the strength God had given Him!

A Radically Real Christian answers the call of God. When you are asked to do something, pray earnestly and ask God for direction. Then, if He gives the go ahead, serve Him faithfully and He will grant you success in His time. Don't automatically write off your lack of ability as a sign that God has not called you. Fifteen years ago, I never would have believed that God would ever call me to the ministry, or for that matter to write a book, but God slowly began to increase my responsibilities at church until I was prepared for where He wants me. Let me tell you something. It is the adventure of a lifetime and I look forward to seeing what God will do next.

Follow

Maybe you were not called to lead, or perhaps you are a leader but in a particular situation, you are not in a position of leadership. What do you do? Radically Real Christians follow faithfully as well. They pray for their leaders and do not interfere unless the leader is taking the church in a direction that is not Biblical. Caution, I said "Biblical" and not "traditional". There is a monumental difference between the two. A Radically Real Christian must never, ever speak the next seven words..."That's the way we've always done it." The Bible never changes because God never changes. That being said, the methods used to reach people may change dramatically. What worked in the 50's may not work in the new millennium. If your leadership is willing to try something new and it is not against the Bible, do yourself a favor. Let them! As a matter of fact, help them. God may have put the idea on their heart. It is vitally important that we pray for our leaders and seek God's wisdom as we serve and then let God be God. Trust Him to do what's right.

Our leaders are ordained by God. We must follow them as such. A person called from above does not need resistance from behind as long as (I'll say it one more time), they are in the will of God. If they are not in the will of God, you will know. If Biblical rules are being violated, if people are being caused to sin, if God would not be pleased, then the leadership is not in the Will of God. Do not judge on numbers!! People leaving a program does not necessarily mean it is a bad program. Some people are resistant to change. Some people will leave if their toes are being righteously stepped on. There is not much you can do about that.

In the church today, a lot of us are more concerned with putting "butts in the seats" than with putting souls in the Kingdom of Heaven. That may sound harsh but if it is not true in your congregation, praise the Lord and hug your pastor. We become more concerned with people being in church so that our attendance numbers look, than with spiritual depth and growth and that has got to stop. Coddling the world does no one any good. It is time for the church and Radically Real Christians everywhere to start speaking the truth in love. This will never be accomplished by sugar coating the Word of God so that the sinners become comfortable in their own "filthy rags" righteousness and miss out on Heaven. If your leaders are leading your church in a Biblical direction, and the numbers are falling, trust God to be faithful. He will bless their efforts. When we are called to follow, Radically Real Christians follow. God will tell us when it is time to stop following. Until then, we must **get out of the way!**

Hot, Cold or Ptewww!

Did you ever get a glass of water that you expected to be ice cold and when you put it in your mouth it was room temperature? Did you like it? Did you ever go to a restaurant and get a steak cut off a piece and put it in your mouth only to discover it was no longer hot? Did you like it? If you are like most people, your answer is an emphatic NO!! It is no different with God. In Revelation 3:15-16, Jesus says, "I know your deeds, that you are neither cold nor hot. I wish that you were either one or the other. So because you are neither cold nor hot, I am about to spit you out of my mouth." What He is saying is this, He would rather have us be hot or cold than lazy, complacent and floating around claiming His name and yet living as if we have no idea what that means.

Some translations say that God will spew out the lukewarm. It basically means that lukewarm Christians make God want to vomit, and with good reason. Christians are supposed to be the light of the world. Lukewarm Christians shine very little, if at all. You can't pick them out of the crowd! As a Radically Real Christian, we are going to write off cold right off the bat. No Radically Real Christian should ever be cold to the Gospel. Radically Real Christians need to be hot! Radically Real Christians need to be fired up!

Radically Real Christians are needed in lukewarm congregations to "heat-up" those who are less excited.

Brothers and sisters in Christ, we have a lot of reason to be fired up! The Creator of the universe loves us enough to send His only son to die for us. We serve a God with unlimited power. We serve a God who has a marvelous plan for our lives. Our Lord listens to, hears and answers our prayers. Even though at times it looks pretty dark, if you look at the end of the book of Revelation you see beyond the shadow of a doubt that we win! Lastly, the main reason to be fired up is that we don't have to go to Hell! We get to spend eternity in Heaven, a paradise that was created for us!

The world is in darkness and it is looking for a light. Radically Real Christian, you are called to be that light. You need to be burning bright. If you are lukewarm maybe you have a little glow but folks won't even see that over the television. God wants you to be a million-candle power spotlight. A lot of the church is going around like a disposable pocket flash-light with the batteries almost dead. Radically Real Christians need to get in there and be that light in the darkness. God also wants us to be like a battery charger to our friends and neighbors around us. Don't worry about losing some of your power in the process. You are plugged into an unending, unbreakable, unlimited power source. So, get out there and shine!

Radically Real People from the Bible

Moses

Moses is a great example of a Radically Real person among the lukewarm. Let's have another look at his life. Right from the start we can see Moses was headed for greatness. He survived Pharaoh's holocaust against the babies of Israel by being hidden in a basket by the river. He was found by Pharaoh's daughter and raised in the splendor of royalty with his own mother as his nurse. Can there be any doubt that even as an infant the hand of God was with Moses? As Moses grew to be a man, he saw a man being beaten by a slave driver. Moses killed the slave driver in defense of the Hebrew slave. Then he had to go into hiding. Moses was a man on the run.

Well, we all know how God called Moses to lead his people from the burning bush and how he felt he was inadequate to do what God had called him to do. In truth he was inadequate to do it just as you are inadequate to do what God has called you to do. It is God working in you that allows you to complete your mission. God makes you adequate just as he did to Moses.

Moses repeatedly went to Pharaoh and asked him to let his people go and each time Pharaoh said no. The Bible says that God hardened Pharaoh's heart and that is why he refused. Why did God harden Pharaoh's heart? Why didn't He just make Pharaoh say, "OK, go ahead and have a nice day?" In the short run, it sure would have made Moses' life a lot easier. But God had a plan.

He knew that the people of Israel needed to see that God had the power to do anything and that He was with Moses. To make a long story short, God was with Moses and with Israel. The most awesome sign of this is when God parted the Red Sea and then dropped it on the Egyptian army. As stated earlier, today some of our "scientists" are trying to explain this miracle away. It takes faith to believe in this kind of "science". The proof is in the word of God!

The children of Israel saw all of this. They saw the plagues fall on Egypt. They saw how they were spared while the people all around them were affected. They saw that when Moses prayed, the plagues went away. They saw God leading them in a pillar of cloud and fire. They saw the Red Sea part and then drown the Egyptian Army. Even after all of this, they still questioned the power of God. They still complained against Moses. As soon as things got a little difficult, they started crying to go back to Egypt. When Moses went up onto the mountain to get the law, the children of Israel heard the voice of God and yet while Moses was on the Mountain they made an idol for themselves to worship. These people were somewhere between ice cold and lukewarm. Their lack of faith, even after having seen all of this, eventually made it so that they had to wander in the desert for forty years.

Moses, through the power of God continued to stay "hot" and he led the people to the edge of the Promised Land. There was at least one time where God became so angry with the people that he was ready to destroy them all and told Moses that he would make of him a great nation. But Moses prayed for the people over and over again. And God stayed with the people.

Radically Real Christians need to be like Moses. The people of today are still seeing God's miracles every day and yet they continue to deny His power and even His existence. We need to stay "hot" just like Moses did. We need to be praying for our friends and neighbors and all the children of God that they might not destroy themselves but rather take the path of salvation. God will be faithful to you just as He was faithful to Moses. You see in the Great Commission, God is calling Christians to lead His people to a new Promised Land. We are called to lead people to Heaven through sharing the Good News of Jesus Christ.

Like Moses, some of us will feel under-qualified and not up to the task, and that is true, but with God there is no good thing we cannot do. Are you up to it? Go with God, Radically Real Christian, go with God!

Chapter 14

Let It Shine!

Living a Radically Real Life

You are the salt of the earth. But if the salt loses its saltiness, how can it be made salty again? It is no longer good for anything, except to be thrown out and trampled by men.

You are the light of the world. A city on a hill cannot be hidden. Neither do people light a lamp and put it under a bowl. Instead they put it on a stand and it gives light to everyone in the house. In the same way, let your light shine before men, that they may see your good deeds and praise your Father in Heaven.

--Matthew 5: 13-16

I have a confession to make. I am a huge rock music fan. I love the sound of screaming guitars. As I began to seek to be Radically Real, I began to have less and less patience for the Godless and anti-God lyrics so prevalent in rock music today. Thank God for the Christian rock bands that go into the world to play their music and reach young people for the Kingdom. I know some people will argue with this statement. They think that "Christian Rock" is a contradiction in terms. I believe that this is more a distaste for the musical style than any legitimate reason. "Christian Rock" is no more a contradiction in terms than "Christian Lawyer", "Christian Politician" or "Christian Public School Teacher". Really all these people are taking the Gospel to the world in places that are hostile to the message at times. They are shining with the light of Jesus into the dark corners of the world. Christian rock musicians have been given their abilities by a loving God, just like people with any other ability. Having met several of them during my time in youth ministry, I never cease to be amazed at the heart for God and for kids these people have.

Whatever your ability is, God has given it to you to use for His glory. Use it, do it, serve Him in the way He designed you for and you will truly be Radically Real. And besides, in the words Larry Norman, "Why Should the Devil Have All the Good Music?"

Too often Christians disagree with the format of someone else's ministry and so rather than letting their light shine, they try to become their neighbor's bushel. Preventing either one from shining, they are too caught up in their own ideas to see the plan of the Lord. Of course, there are people out there that are doing wrong things in their ministry and we should definitely be vigilant. If we see a brother or sister going astray, that is one thing. It is quite another if we simply find their way of ministry different and since we never did it that way before, we "rain on their parade." God's Will is never sin, PERIOD. If a person tries to convince you he is a Crack Dealer for Christ, clearly they are outside the will of God. Lead them back to the straight and narrow and pray for them. If on the other hand he is an ex-crack dealer that is now going out on the streets working with kids strung out on drugs, do not get in his way. His life has been changed by Christ and now the Lord is using him in this way. Pray for him that he may not fall to temptation and support him. He is seeking to be Radically Real.

One of my favorite Christian Rock Bands is the Newsboys. They do a song called "Shine". The chorus of the song encourages Christians to shine in such a way that the rest of the world is drawn to the joy in your life. Radically Real Christians must live with a faith that people can see.

I believe this song, which is based on Matthew 5:14-16, listed earlier in this chapter, shows a key to letting your light shine in a Radically Real way. The first part talks about what I call "lifestyle evangelism." Basically, this means living a righteous and joyous lifestyle and making people wonder how you do it. A person who is in the darkness of sin or depression will see the way you live and be impressed, even if they don't show it. They may act like they enjoy the life they are in, or they may actually be enjoying it--but sin eventually hurts and when it does, they will remember you and how joyous you were, and wonder why. Be ready to tell them. A word of caution here: "Lifestyle evangelism" is not enough. If people see your life and you never tell them about Jesus, they will assume that you are just a good person and that puts the glory in the wrong place. Similarly spoken evangelism is not enough, because your actions will always speak louder than your words. The key is to do both.

The second part of the chorus deals with letting it shine before all men. This does not mean we go around grabbing for God's glory (Satan did that and we can all see where it got him). What it does mean is that we live our Christian walk publicly. No beating around the bush allowed. If you shine behind closed doors and in the world are indistinguishable from anyone else, you do not glorify God. Radically Real Christians always seek to shine. So how do we shine?

I can think of three components that probably sum it up:

Righteous living:

There are many Biblical calls to righteousness that we really should examine. In this volume we are going to consider four. Some of this will appear to be rehashed, but it is of the utmost importance that we really consider righteousness, since it is such a large part of what it means to be Radically Real. Essentially these four "audiences" watch our every move.

God is watching: *What shall we say then? Shall we go on sinning that grace may increase? By no means! We died to sin; how can we live in it any longer? (Romans 6:1,2 NIV)*

All Christians are saved by the grace of God. None of us is deserving of the Salvation He offered us in Jesus, but He did it anyway because he loves us. My pastor has an interesting acronym for Grace: God's Riches at Christ's Expense. If we persist in our sins after we accept Christ's gift of salvation, we are in effect spitting on the sacrifice Jesus made for us. All of us will slip up, and we can be forgiven, but we should at all times be resisting the temptation to sin. To be Radically Real, we should live a life that is pleasing to God out of sheer gratitude. We deserved Hell, but instead we were given eternal life in heaven. If someone told you, you would get an all-expense paid trip to Hawaii if you just were able to avoid your "favorite sin" for a period of time, would you do it? I know this much, you would try, really, really hard. Well Radically Real Christian, you do have an all-expense paid trip coming up, guaranteed to a place that is much better than Hawaii. What better reason is there to try and live a righteous life? Live as if God is watching (because He is) and you will live a life that gives Him glory.

The world is watching: *You are the Light of the World...(Matthew 5: 14-16 see above)*

Jesus refers to us as the light of the world. What a great analogy, look at the world around you. Darkness is everywhere. People are in despair. People are hopeless. People are falling into trap after trap after trap, because they cannot see the danger that is right in front of their faces. Their whole world is dark. And then one day they see you. You are shining because you call upon the name of Jesus. They notice a difference in you and they start to watch. They cannot help but watch. They are drawn to you like moths to a light. They want your hope. They want desperately to see that you are for real.

The problem comes is this, if we call upon the name of the Lord and people are drawn to us, we have a responsibility to continue to walk in the light. If we begin to sin, they will see that too. And when they see that, we have turned from a light they are drawn to, to being a warning light chasing them away from our Lord. You see they begin to look at you and think you are a fraud and a hypocrite and if you are not real, then surely your God cannot be real either. Radically Real Christian, do not become a stumbling block to the very people you were called to reach. They need to find Jesus. They need you to light the way. The only way you can do that is to stay connected to your "power source" and being the light that leads them home.

Your brothers and sisters in Christ are watching: "Be careful, however, that the exercise of your freedom does not become a stumbling block to the weak. For if anyone with a weak conscience sees you who have this knowledge eating in an idol's temple, won't he be emboldened to eat what has been sacrificed to idols? So this weak brother, for whom Christ died, is destroyed by your knowledge. When you sin against your brothers in this way, and wound their weak conscience, you sin against Christ. Therefore, if what I eat causes my brother to fall into sin, I will never eat meat again, so that I will not cause him to fall." 1 Corinthians 8:9-13 (NIV)

Paul, who I believe is one of the finest examples of a Radically Real Christian in all of the Scriptures, gives us a warning. We are not to live in such a way that it would cause a brother or sister in Christ, especially a weaker one to stumble. He is referring here to food offered to idols. Many of the people Paul reached out to as he evangelized were former idolaters. Basically, what Paul is saying is that even though he as a Christian saw the idol as a powerless piece of rock, if seeing him eat meat offered to it would cause one of these new believers to fall away, he would rather not eat the meat.

Paul is giving us a great example here. You see how we act can make others feel free to sin. If we are a Christian, if we claim the name of Jesus, we had better be prepared to live like it so that we do not cause others to fall away. One thing that comes to mind is drinking alcohol. To some Christians, the act of drinking alcohol is not a sin. They interpret the verse that says, "be ye not drunk with wine," to mean that they are free to drink alcohol as long as they do not get drunk. There is certainly some truth to that statement, however, I choose abstinence and would encourage others to do the same. I would never want to be an example that would cause someone to sin. To my mind it is better that I abstain.

The example goes even further. People are watching the way we live. Many people will even look up to you, especially if you are living a Radically Real life. Even if you are always careful to give the glory to God, you become a role model. Radically Real Christians are always to remember that they represent Jesus and should live as He lived. We must constantly and prayerfully consider how our actions affect others, especially our brothers and sisters in Christ. We must be willing to speak the truth in love to a brother or sister that is going astray. Likewise, we must be willing to accept the correction of a brother or sister in Christ. In this way we will always be ready to be Radically Real.

The children are watching: *"If anyone causes one of these little ones who believe in me to sin, it would be better for him to have a millstone hung around his neck and be drowned in the depths of the sea" --Matthew 18:6 (NIV)*

As a youth worker, my least favorite saying in the entire English language is "kids today..." The reason for this is because that phrase is almost always followed by some negative statement about them and the way they act or the way they live. The fact of the matter is "kids today" live in the world we have created. I am not referring to the God's creation. I am referring to the sin we have thrust upon his creation. They live in broken homes and messed up families. The divorce rate is over 50%. They have ready access to all the sex and violence they could ever imagine in the media. Did you know that by the time a kid graduates from high school they have seen 70,000 murders on TV alone? Even the sitcoms are pushing the envelope on language and content on a daily basis. Premarital sex is glorified and accepted as a rite of passage. I won't even get into MTV, although if you are a parent and you want a good idea on the music your kids may be listening to check out www.philchalmers.com.

The truth of the matter is our kids are swimming in a moral cesspool and we wonder why they don't come out of it smelling like a rose. Maybe it is because I am a parent and a youth worker, but I really feel that this is the most important call to righteousness for the Radically Real Christian.

You see our kids are looking for role models and they are looking for boundaries. They are in larger numbers everyday looking for someone to lead them in the right direction. It is pretty obvious from what Jesus had to say on the subject that we had better get this one right. Let's face it there are a lot of people in the world today that ought to be fitted for millstones. "Do as I say not as I do" is a joke and a cruel one at that. We need to realize that what we do is what they will do.

If we tell them worship is important and that God should be the most important thing in their life and then turn around and let them skip worship for every activity that rolls down the pike what are we really showing them? Likewise, if we skip church every time something "better" comes along (even our jobs) what are we really showing them? Remember we are talking about modeling a radical commitment here. The fact of the matter is the kids will model our priorities. There is a reason God created the world in six days and rested on the seventh. My next statement will cause much resistance and upset many. If your job requires you to work on the Lord's day, quit. There are enough non-Christians in the world to cover those positions. Now I know that there are a few essential positions that need to be done seven days a week, medical and public safety for example, but even in those fields a concerted effort to worship with our families should be a top priority. The kids are watching.

Radically Real Christians have to be training their kids in the ways of the Lord both in word and deed. We have to live the example. Parents who drink in front of their kids will have kids who drink. Don't even try to tell me about them being too young but that it is OK for you. You can sell that somewhere else if you want to but don't even try to sell it here. The behavior a parent models, is the behavior they will get. Parents who swear will have kids that swear. Parents who are violent have kids who are violent. You are a role model.

Parents who spend time in the Word of God will have kids that spend time in the Word of God. The Bible tells us to train up a child in the way he should go and when he is old he will not depart from it. The foundation we give our kids is the one they will build on. Don't depend on the church to give your kids their spiritual training. First of all, some of the churches aren't doing all that great at it. The Bible has fallen behind social issues in a whole lot of churches, and rather than showing what the Bible has to say and how it is relevant to the situation, man-made solutions are being preached from the pulpits.

The other reason you cannot depend on the church to do the spiritual training is simply a matter of time. As a youth worker, I can really relate to this. Even with my most committed kids, I only get about three hours a week to get them into the Word of God. That is nowhere near enough. By way of comparison, they get 30 hours a week of school, 15 hours a week in from of the TV (if that covers it). We in the church need your help if you are a parent or even someone that comes in contact with kids.

Christian teachers are limited to what they can do in the public schools. That's OK. We would rather have them there planting all the little seeds you can get away with. The rest of us need to be really supportive of our Christian Teachers. We need to give them the benefit of the doubt. They are in a tough mission field. We need to pray for them and we need more people to take up this mission. I have spent entire youth meetings refuting atheistic teachings my kids have picked up in school. I am not just talking about evolution either. I am talking about teachers that teach deliberately to make kids question their Christian faith.

You see make no mistake about it, the separation of church and state applies only to Christianity. (Incidentally, I defy anyone to show me the words separation of church and state in the constitution, that is another story for another book). If you have the gift of teaching, use it, to God's glory. Be a light in the public schools. Teach in a Christian school. Go to a mission school. Our kids need Christian examples in the schools. They need you.

Make no mistake about it, if we were to take the above passage literally, there would be a line at the millstone shop around the block. The truth is though, that those may be some of the strongest words Jesus ever used in His earthly ministry. The children are very special to Him. We had better focus our efforts on helping the little ones to come to him. As Jesus said in

Matthew 19:14, "Let the little children come to me and DO NOT HINDER THEM (emphasis mine), for the Kingdom of Heaven belongs to such as these." (NIV) He also reminds us, just before the verse used to open this section that whoever welcomes a child in His name, welcomes Him. I think we can see the value Jesus places on kids and we had better do the same.

Kids have an answer for everything, it seems, but the truth of the matter is they have questions about everything. We cannot just tell them. We have to show them. Radically Real Christians must live in a way that leads the kids they come in contact with, down the right road. When it appears they have chosen the wrong road, we cannot write them off. We have to be there for them and help them back to the right road. Sooner or later sin loses its luster and then they will remember your example and turn to the right road. Pray for "kids today". They have it rough.

Good Works: First off, let me make it clear, salvation is by faith. You cannot earn your way into heaven. As Paul tells us in Ephesians 2: 8,9, "For it is by grace you have been saved, through faith--and this is not from yourselves, it is the gift of God--not by works, so that no one can boast." (NIV) It is by the grace of God that we are saved, period. None of us is capable of doing enough good to buy our own Salvation. We need Jesus and his gift of salvation to enter the kingdom of heaven. This verse, however, is not an excuse for spiritual laziness. Just because we cannot earn our way into heaven does not mean there is not work to be done. As a matter of fact, if we go on to the next verse we see the following: "For we are God's workmanship, created in Christ Jesus to do good works which God prepared in advance for us to do." As part of God's plan, we were created to do specific good works. Now, he has given us free will to decide whether or not we will do them, but a Radically Real Christian always seeks to do the Will of God and fulfill God's plan for our lives. We must seek to do our part in His perfect plan.

As has been stated before, each of us has been gifted with abilities to do the things God has planned for us. Everything people ask us to do is not necessarily the calling of God. We must discern what things God is calling us to do. This comes from prayer and not just a quick "off the cuff" decision. We cannot do everything and God is not calling us to do everything. We must however not automatically write off certain things because we feel inadequate. God does not always allow us to dwell in our comfort zone. Remember, "I can do all things through Christ who gives me strength." I never thought I would ever preach; I avoided public speaking like the plague and today I preach. God is faithful and He will give you what you need to complete your mission.

Success does not always follow serving God, or more precisely earthly success. You may not see the fruits of your labors. This is in no way an excuse to quit. If you reach out to a person to witness, for example, and they reject what you had to say, the response of many is to say I am no good at it and quit. Feelings of failure can be real, but often they are a lie from the pit of Hell. I think back to my paternal grandmother, who for years told me she prayed for me and told me about Jesus while I was on the wrong road. She was always very loving about it and yet, I more or less "blew it off." I loved her (and still do) but I really figured her beliefs were kind of old fashioned. She never quit!

When living the world's way had taken its toll on me years later, I had these "nagging" recollections of things that she had said to me and eventually her words helped me to come to Christ. You see she modeled a steadfast faith and there came a time in my life when I could no longer avoid the fact that she had been right all along. I praise God that a few weeks ago, I got a chance to stand in the pulpit and publicly thank her and she got to hear me preach. She lived to see her prayers answered and answered abundantly. That's what God does when we serve Him faithfully. He always exceeds our expectations. We may not see it in this life, but in the end through his grace and the gift of salvation, we will see it.

James goes even a bit further in his call for us to do good works. He tells us, through the inspiration of the Holy Spirit that faith without works is dead. You see I believe that works are an act of gratitude. They are way of saying thank you for all the many things that God has done for us. Good works are a small token for the great blessings of God. We can never repay him, our debt is too large, but we can do all we can to serve His Kingdom. If you have faith and you do nothing, can anyone "see your good works and praise your Father in heaven" as we see back in Matthew 5:16? Of course you can't. People cannot see that you have faith if you do nothing. At the same time if we do good works and do not attribute them to God, God is not glorified. It is the combination of faith and good works that brings glory to God. That is the purpose in life for every Christian, especially the Radically Real Believer.

Witness and Evangelism: We have already had some discussion on this, but it bears repeating. If people don't know why you're shining, you become a false source of light. Like the moon that has no power to shine on its own, we have no power to shine, without the light of Jesus living in us. It is vitally important that as we begin to shine that we always remember to give credit where credit is due. If we don't give glory to God for the good things we do, how will anyone come to know Him? Radically Real Christians are called to live a life of radical commitment to giving glory to God. We cannot do that if folks see our good works and praise only us.

A natural extension of this is evangelism. It is the step we take to try, in the Holy Spirit, to lead people to Jesus. This is not only done in crusades folks. An awful lot of evangelism is done one to one, friend to friend. Sometimes people from outside the church have a hard time believing what's in the Bible. Let's face it, the power of God to do things like parting seas, world-wide floods, a whale swallowing a prophet, etc., without a belief and faith in Him sound like fairy tales. People are skeptical.

Some people have also been really turned off by the constant bickering that seems to be occurring between people and denominations. People want to see Jesus as real; they want that hope and there is one thing that no skeptic can disbelieve and that is the fervent witness of one whose heart has been changed by Jesus Christ. Notice I said fervent. That means a strong persistent witness. We do not necessarily beat them over the head with it, but we do tell them at every opportunity God gives us. Remember, it is the Holy Spirit that actually takes our witness and uses it to touch lives, we just need to be faithful and never give up. I recently spoke to a friend of mine, Joe. He was filled with joy like I have never seen him before (and that is saying something because few people possess the joy that Joe does). If you were to look up Radically Real Christian in the dictionary the picture beside it would be Joe. Joe related a story to me. His cousin had just given his life to Jesus after, get this, 21 years of prayer and witnessing. You can never give up on someone until they close the box. God works on us in his own time, but He never stops working and neither can we.

Let Your Light Shine! We have already spoken a lot about shining, but just remember this; your actions will always shine brighter than your words and nothing can dull your light more than not "practicing what you preach." While none of us will reach perfection on this side of the grave, we must strive to reflect the light of Jesus at all times. A mistake must always be followed by a quick and heartfelt apology, atonement and restitution. It means that we must be willing to turn the other cheek even at times when it is most difficult. It means that we must react in the way that is unexpected by the world and when the world sees we are different we must be prepared to tell them why. Letting our light shine is where the "rubber meets the road-

-is the Radically Real lifestyle. Bottom line, it is the way that people will see you are for real.

Breaking the Bushels! "Hide it under a bushel, NO, I'm gonna let it shine." So goes the children's Sunday school song, but it bears repeating. Our light does no good if it is hidden. We need to put off the bushels. There is no room for shame in the Radically Real Christian's "game." As Jesus put it, whoever acknowledges me before men, I will acknowledge him before my father in heaven. It is time for us to throw off the bushels and shine bright for Jesus. What does that mean? For starters it means that we have to be bold about our faith. We have to go into the world and tell people. We have to help the hurting, the needy and anyone else and we need to tell them that reason we did what we did is because of Jesus. It means we go to the sinners, the sick, the outcasts and the weak just like Jesus did. It means we live like Jesus has made a difference in our lives. It means we are quick to acknowledge our own sin and our own weakness and our own need for Jesus. It means that we use God's blessings to bless others. The world is looking for the hope that Jesus offers, we are the light of the world. Like a lighthouse on a rocky shore, we need to shine and help to guide people safely home.

The bushels in our lives are the things that separate us from God and make our witness null and void. It is time for them to go! Every day of our lives should be an exercise in getting closer and closer to God. We need to pray and be in the Word daily. We need to look for ways to serve Him daily. Often, we serve Him by serving each other. If we do this, we will shine brighter each and every day. The bushels will be gone and the world will "see our good deeds and praise our father in heaven." Smash the bushels and shine!

Help Your Church Be A City on A Hill: Some time, bring a Christian friend to church. It has to be someone unknown to the rest of the congregation. Split up and ignore them as if you don't know them and watch. Are your brothers and sisters warm to your friend? Are they inviting? Do they make your friend feel at home? If we are not warm to strangers in our midst, we do a great disservice to the Lord. A person should feel as welcome in your church as they do in their own home (and in some cases even more welcome).

We also must go beyond the walls of our churches if we truly want to be a light to our communities. We need to not only invite people to our services and share our faith as mentioned in previous chapters, but we must also be meeting the needs of our community. A BIG word of caution here: when we serve, we must always serve in the name of Jesus Christ. Our purpose is to bring glory to God at all times. If people look at our churches, they might see a bunch of nice people instead of people who serve an awesome God. They might join us as one would join the Rotary Club. Now, don't get me wrong, the Rotary Club is a great organization and their service to the community is awesome. But what I am saying is that the church is not a club, the church is the body of Christ and sharing the Gospel is the church's primary purpose. Service is a means to that end, not the church's purpose.

I can illustrate this point from a congregation that I know pretty well. A few years back, they had a man of great importance to the community begin to attend their services. They were excited to have him. In addition to the fact that they had a new brother in the congregation, he had a lot of abilities and connections that could have really opened up their ministry. We could say he brought a lot of God's blessings to the table. After two or three weeks he stopped attending. The pastor finally caught up with him and asked him why he had stopped attending, and he said that He was attracted to the church because of their position on peace and because of their community service, but the preaching was a bit too "conservative". I have heard this pastor preach on many occasions and have always found him to be very loving, very humble and very Biblical. This man was looking for a club or a service organization, not a church.

To be a city on a hill does not take a lot of money, but it does take people who are willing to shine with the light of Christ. It takes a lot of prayer and a lot of effort. It is crucial, however, to make sure that the effort is guided by prayer. It is not enough to be busy. We must be led by the Spirit. It also doesn't take the hot new thing or some elaborate program (though by all means use all the gifts and abilities that God has blessed you with). A good example of this is our church's Vacation Bible School. Lots of people work very hard to put it together, but it is hardly reinventing the wheel. We have done it for years and years. People from all over the community bring their children for one week of evenings over the summer and at the end we have a program where the students can show what they learned and an Ice Cream social afterwards. Every year a few new families join our congregation as a result.

If I had to pick a slogan for a church that will become a "city on a hill", it would be very simply this, "Love thy neighbor". We live in a world where people are looking for love. They are looking for authenticity and people who say what they mean and mean what they say. They are looking for people that are Radically Real (That is why I wrote this book). They are looking for a warm greeting and a friendly smile. They are looking for a place where they will be accepted and challenged. But most of all they are looking for the truth. What greater truth is there than the truth of Jesus Christ. Can we really say we love our neighbor if we don't share the truth of Jesus. I think not. The time has long past for "Sunday Christians". We need to be Christians 24-7 if we are going to reach this world. If the church is going to be truly effective, all the members must be using their God given gifts to the best of their ability and we must model our faith in every aspect of our lives. Radically Real Churches will shine as bright as the sun in this dark world if we are all working together and in concert with our Lord. It's kind of like the motel chain's commercial, "Do you have the light on for them?"

Radically Real People from the Bible

The Angels

OK, once again, I know that the angels are not actually people, but they are beings made by God to serve His purposes and so their actions are worthy of our consideration as we look at shining for the Lord. The first thing I want to say is this, no angel of the Lords will ever accept our worship. No angel of the Lord in the Bible ever accepts worship, except The Angel of the Lord, which is thought not to really be an angel but rather a Old Testament manifestation of Jesus. If we look at the book of Revelation, we see a stunned and amazed John, twice fall at the feet of the angel who is guiding Him through his vision. Both times the angel tells him to rise to his feet because the angel is a servant of the Lord just like John is. Angels are worshippers and are not to be worshipped.

In the world today, there are people that worship angels. They refer to them as ascended masters or spirit guides or they just plain pray to their guardian angels. This is very clearly, 100% wrong. The angels are God's servants, just like we are. We exist just like they do, to glorify God and worship Him only! An angel that accepts worship, is Satanic, period. Do not fall into the trap. Angels are also not dead people, or more specifically, they are not the spirits of people that have gone before. They are created beings that serve the Father. While we do not become angels, we do have a lot in common. There are also some glaring differences however and the chief among them is this. They do not experience salvation. The angels that fell with Lucifer are condemned for all eternity. That is why they struggle so hard to drag us down with them.

Let's look at what the angels do. We see that they are messengers. The angel came to Zechariah, to tell Him He would become a father to John the Baptist in his old age. An angel told a teenaged Mary that she would be the mother of God. An angel told Joseph that it was OK to take the pregnant

Mary as his wife because the child was of the Holy Spirit. An angel also went to Joseph and told him to flee into Egypt. These are just a few of many times the angels served as messengers from God. You have a message from God for the people too. It is called the Word of God. It is called the Gospel of Jesus, the message of Salvation. When we shine for the Lord, we become messengers of the Good News. It is our calling.

The angels also do battle against the forces of Darkness. Radically Real Christians, how can you and I battle the forces of evil? It is very simple. Darkness is defeated by light. When we shine with the light of Jesus, when we go into battle against evil with our armor on and stand firm behind Jesus, victory is ours. Lies are defeated by the truth. It is up to us to share the truth. When Christians shine the light of truth, the darkness has no choice but to flee. We must stand firm. Like any war, there will be times when we feel defeated, but we must rest assured that the end is already determined and we are on the winning team. Think about the way the disciples felt when Jesus hung on that cross. They felt crushed, defeated, and very, very scared. And then one day Jesus came through the locked door and they realized that they were undefeatable in Him. Not even death could beat them and they left that place and went boldly into the world. Christian it's the same way with us.

Think about the time in your life when you realized that you needed Jesus. For some you have been trained up from your childhood to know you needed Him. If that's you, praise the Lord, He has blessed you richly. For others, we found Jesus when we were so defeated that the only way left to look was up. It was then that Jesus came to the door and knocked and we let Him in. It was then that we realized that it is all true. Where once we were defeated by the world, now we can stand against it in Him. Radically Real Christian, when we shine the light of Jesus into a dark world, victory is at hand.

One of the chief things that Angels do is worship. We see them surrounding the throne of God and praising Him for all eternity. One day we get to do that too. Saved from the darkness of the world, we will be perfected and we will bow down before our Creator and praise Him for the great things He has done in our lives. Brothers and sisters, that will be a glorious day. We will be part of a great multitude, a multitude of men, women and angels who have seen the magnificent, amazing power and grace of our Heavenly Father.

As I consider the angels and I consider the Christians that I love who have gone home to Heaven, I am always reminded of Luke 15:10. "In the same way there is rejoicing before the angels of God when one sinner repents." (NIV) When any sinner comes to Christ (remember all have sinned and fallen short of the glory of God) and puts their sin behind them, it is time for a wild celebration in heaven. I can almost see the angels and the saints uproariously worshipping God for yet another victory over the evil one. Folks, God is worthy of all our praise. He truly is a great and awesome God. His victory is apparent in the changed lives of people all over the world. How can we that claim His name not shine brightly with His light?

Angels are not mentioned very much in the Bible, after Pentecost, (at least not until John's guide in the book of Revelation.) That does not mean they ceased to work or exist. They are still out there doing the work of the Lord. It is very simply now, that rather than having the angels to guide us, we have God Himself living in our hearts and guiding us from within. You see when we have His Holy Spirit, we are truly in the presence of God at all times. What better source of light is there than God? I mean think about it, He said let there be light on the first day of Creation, and He never made the sun until the fourth day. Before that He, Himself was the Light. He still is and He wants to shine through us. What better reason is there to be Radically Real?

Chapter 15

RU4 Real?

What About It, Are You Radically Real?

Jesus answered, "I am the way and the truth and the life. No one comes to the Father except through me. If you really knew me you would know my Father as well. From now on, you do know Him and have seen Him."

--John 14: 6,7

Well, you've read the book and you've seen part of what it means to be Radically Real. In writing this book I have become painfully aware of how much I have missed. Like John, in the end of the book of John, I begin to doubt that all the books in the World would be adequate to cover the impact Jesus has on our lives. If the Lord is willing, there will be more books by me and many others far more worthy. There will be books on spiritual disciplines, on prayer and on worship that while, touched on here can only really be properly covered in books of their own. It is my hope that this book will be used to draw people closer to God. Of course this is not the ultimate book on the subject. That title would be reserved for the Word of God. Read it and apply it to your life.

In the meantime, though, let's see how you are doing. Let's see if you are for real. The first section is on the physical evidence. You know, the stuff you can see. It is meant for you to grade yourself. Through it, you can see where you need to work.

The second section is the Spiritual evidence. That's the stuff that only you and God can see. Both of these dimensions are very important. They are sometimes diagrammed as a cross. The horizontal bar represents our relationship with our fellow man and the vertical bar represents our relationship with God. To be Radically Real, both relationships must be in proper alignment.

Of course, in order for either or both to be in perfect alignment is humanly impossible. But as we seek God's help, if we seek the face and the Will of God, we come closer to the way God wants us to be. And the closer we come to God the closer we come to being Radically Real. It's this simple really, only God is perfect. If you wait until you are perfect to start to serve the Lord, you will never start. Your imperfections do not make you a hypocrite. They make you human. They make you real. Trust the Lord, reach out with the love of Jesus and be real about your imperfections and you will be effective in serving the Lord. You will be Radically Real.

Are you ready for the test? Let's go!!

RU4REAL?

If it were illegal to be a Christian, would there be enough evidence to convict you?

PART ONE

The Physical Evidence

Rate yourself on the following from 1-10 (10 being the highest)

People can tell I'm a Christian by the way I act

1   2   3   4   5   6   7   8   9   10

People can tell I'm a Christian by the things I do

1   2   3   4   5   6   7   8   9   10

People can tell I'm a Christian by the things I wear

1   2   3   4   5   6   7   8   9   10

People can tell I'm a Christian by the way I treat them

1   2   3   4   5   6   7   8   9   10

People can tell I'm a Christian by my lifestyle

1   2   3   4   5   6   7   8   9   10

People can tell I'm a Christian by my priorities

1   2   3   4   5   6   7   8   9   10

People can tell I'm a Christian by the places I go

1   2   3   4   5   6   7   8   9   10

People can tell I'm a Christian by my choices

1   2   3   4   5   6   7   8   9   10

PART TWO

The Physical Evidence

Jesus commanded us to be salt and light. This means we are to "let our light shine" if Jesus is making a difference in our lives. (If you are breathing, He is.) How are you letting your light shine?

____

____

____

"Hide it under a bushel, NO, I'm gonna let it shine." What are the "bushels in your life that are keeping your light from shining through?

____

____

____

What are you going to do about it?

____

____

____

Jesus told Nicodemus and us that you must be born again. Paul tells us that, "if any man is in Christ, He is a new Creation, the old is gone and the new is come." What evidence do you have that you are a new creation?

____

____

____

Jesus tells us to be "living sacrifices". He also tells us we must take up our cross and follow Him. What have you sacrificed for the Lord?

____

____

____

If you don't know, what are you going to do about it?

____

____

____

Jesus tells us that men will know we are His disciples by the way we love one another. How can people tell you are one of His disciples? (Be specific.)

____

____

____

____

____

____

We are instructed in the scriptures to be imitators of Christ. How can you do that?

____

____

____

If you don't know, what are you going to do about it?

____

____

____

Jesus tells us He will never leave us nor forsake us; He also tells us that we can come to Him when we are weary and heavy-laden and He will give us rest. When you are faced with a struggle what do you do?

____

____

____

If you don't know, what are you going to do about it?

____

____

____

Jesus tells us that we will be forgiven as we forgive. He also tells us that all have sinned and fallen short of the glory of God. When someone wrongs you, how do you react?

____

____

____

If you are forgiven as you forgive, will you be forgiven?

____

____

____

The Bible tells us that the Word of God is a lamp unto our feet and a light unto our path. Do you go to the Word of God to find your answers?

____

Why or why not?

____

____

____

What do you need to do to improve your time in the Word?

____

____

____

The Bible tells us that we are either for Christ or against Him. How can people tell who's side you're on?

____

____

____

Jesus tells us that where our treasure is, there our heart will be also. Where is your heart? (Be honest) Where is your number one priority?

____

____

____

If you don't know, what are you going to do about it?

____

____

____

____

There is an old saying, "People don't care how much you know until they know how much you care." How do people know how much you care?

____

____

____

____

If you don't know, what are you going to do about it?

____

____

____

Jesus tells us to go into all the world spreading the Gospel. He also tells us that no one gets to heaven without Him. Do you know for sure, beyond the shadow of a doubt that you are going to heaven?

_______________________ (If you answered "no" you can be sure, just pray the prayer in chapter 3.)

What are you going to do to make sure that everyone you know is going to hears the Gospel

____

____

____

____

Pray and ask God to help you to come up with a detailed plan.

____

____

____

____

____

____

____

____

____

____

A Final Word

To sum up the message of this book in a few words, I would simply say that a Radically Real Christian lives their life with the hope of one day hearing their Father say, "well done!" Put another way, the Radically Real Christian strives to live a transparent life so that when the world sees you, they can look right through you and see Jesus. It is a worthy goal for any Christian and I truly believe that if you seek God continually, you cannot help but become Radically Real.

A Radically Real Christian is not a perfect person, nor do they ever pretend to be. No, we should do our best in Christ to live His example and take comfort in the words of Paul, who reminded us that God's strength is revealed in our weakness. Show the world your struggles, show them your failings, but also show them the hope and joy and peace you have in knowing

Jesus Christ. If you can do this you will be a Christian with a magnetic faith, a light in a dark world. In short, you will be Radically Real.

Remember, one day we will all stand before the throne of grace. We will fall to our face in the presence of sheer perfection. I believe we will tremble before the Lord. I know that every knee will bow and every tongue will confess. And then as we lie prostrate before the throne, we will feel a hand on our shoulder, a hand that on some level we will recognize, an imperfect hand in a place of sheer an utter perfection, a hand with a scar, the imperfection by which you were made perfect in the eyes of God, the hand of Jesus Christ. He will help you to your feet. You may still hesitate to look him in the eye so he gently places a finger under your chin to pull your eyes to His. You see the love that has transcended all time. He speaks with the voice that spoke the world into existence. "Well done, good and faithful servant. Welcome home."

If you enjoyed this author's book, then please place a review up at the site of purchase, and any social media sites you frequent!

You can find ALL our books up on our website at:

https://www.writers-exchange.com

All our Christian Books:

https://www.writers-exchange.com/category/genres/christian/

About the Author

David C. Weiss is a speaker, minister, youth leader and a Christian struggling to be radically real.

He is a member of the WriteGroup for the youth ministry resource, Interlinc, writing Bible studies based on the themes of Contemporary Christian Music. He has written several youth ministry electronic guidebooks and writes a bi-weekly evangelism column called "The GO Zone" on http://www.crosshome.com. A graphic designer/cartoonist by trade, he is the founder of A.M.O.K. (Arts Ministry Outreach for the Kingdom), a ministry dedicated to creating resources to help people in ministry use the arts as an outreach tool. He is married with two sons and resides in the middle of a cornfield in Mohrsville, Pennsylvania.

For more on Radically Real and David's ministry check out http://www.radicallyreal.com